Asian Giants in Indian Works

A Compendium of References

B.K. Kumar

B.R. Publishing Corporation
[A Division of BRPC (India) Ltd.]
Delhi-110035

Distributed by:
BRPC (India) Ltd.
4222/1, Ansari Road, Darya Ganj,
New Delhi-110002
Ph.: 3259196, 3259648
Fax: 3201571
E-Mail: *brpcltd @ del2.vsnl.net.in*

ISBN 81-7646-089-3

Published by:
B.R. Publishing Corporation
[A Division of BRPC (India) Ltd]
3779, Ist Floor, Kanhaiya Nagar,
Tri Nagar, Delhi-110035
Phone: 7152140
E-Mail: *brpcltd @ del2.vsnl.net.in*

Rs. 360.00

Laser Typeset by:
Divya Computers
New Delhi

Printed at:
PRAJA Offset
Delhi

PRINTED IN INDIA

For Professor Kashi Ram Sharma and Dr. Brij Tankha in gratitude of their sustained support and partonage to the Chinese and Japanese Studies Documentation Programme.

For M.L. Saini, Delhi University Librarian, in approbation of his torch-bearer's role played in computerising and modernising the DULS information and library services.

FOREWORD

The last decade has been one of extensive and prolific writing and research on East Asia by Indian researchers, academics and writers. For some time now, the need for a systematic and organized compendium of all this material has been rather obvious and gaining in urgency—a volume which would assist research scholars in locating their requirements without delay and, more importantly, tell them where to locate it. Furthermore, in this era of fast-paced technological developments, such documentation is of immense benefit.

Mr. B.K. Kumar, in his *Asian Giants in Indian Works* Vision 2001, has done yeoman's service to documentation services generally, and to the arena of compiling works on China and Japan particularly. The subjects covered are diverse: ranging from international relations to comparative studies to cuisine, and from rural and gender studies to problems of modernization and liberalization.

This volume is the first part of Mr. Kumar's work, which includes whole books and research theses related to Chinese and Japanese Studies. The second part will hopefully include research articles and papers and some of the more important and significant journalistic coverage on China and Japan. Apart from the specialized journals, I hope, that journals such as *Economic and Political Weekly*, which are extremely representative of contemporary social science and area studies in India, will get a place of prominence in Mr. Kumar's forthcoming compilation.

New Delhi
May 25, 1999

G.P. Deshpande
Professor and former Dean
School of International Studies
Jawaharlal Nehru University
New Delhi

PREFACE

India's interaction with two of the predominant nations of East Asia, China and Japan, in consonance with the world-wide acceptance of the phenomenon of globalisation and openness, has been uniformly strengthened in the socio-economic, cultural and political fields during the last few decades. Concomitantly, the complex turn and twist of events in the economic and political arena, in particular as observed in the first half of the present decade and beyond, has not only thrown up new approaches available for more systematic exploration of the existing framework of inquiry but also illuminated new paths of inquiry.

It was in the context of this newly emerging radicalised subject (or interdisciplinary) scenario that bibliographic exploration of the place of the two East Asian giants of the century in wide-ranging publications emanating from all parts of India seemed to evoke a sense of new urgency and interest among the world-wide community of scholars and area specialists concerned. Also, as a byproduct of an on-going indexing project on China and Japan under way at the Department of Chinese and Japanese Studies, University of Delhi, the exercise held out the prospects of commanding exclusive and expeditious academic interest.

Thus it was realised that the task of scanning over seven thousand Indian publications every year to collect references on China and Japan as a part of the overall indexing project has in fact assumed the proportions of an independent project after an *indexing span of more than five years*. And it was, therefore, decided that the fruit of this project must be made available for the use of the scholars concerned with speed and in the form of a manageable quantity of references. In order to achieve the first objective, that is, 'speed', the famous Indian Journal on East Asia called *China Report*, rendered a commendable support: by publishing a part of the bibliographic compilation in *three of its issues*. Further, to achieve the second objective—'manageable quantity'—(together with the first), the entire work of the decade in question was contemplated to be split up into *two Parts*.

The first Part, that is, the present work, covers the Indian publications brought out during the period, 1990-96 and beyond, which include whole books and research theses related to Chinese or Japanese Studies, and relevant chapters or sections in composite works unrelated to China or Japan: which in fact in themselves form a predominant segment of this work.

Three points in connection with the above-mentioned exercise need to be made clear. One, the indexing undertaken for purposes of this work has excluded from the purview the reprints or the revised editions of publications which were originally published in the earlier years. Two, the periodicals/serials, which form an important component of the total indexing endeavour, have been completely excluded. Three, the entire concentration has been placed on the publications released from India irrespective of the nationality of the author concerned.

B.K. Kumar

ACKNOWLEDGEMENTS

This project which in itself is a byproduct of the larger indexing project on Chinese and Japanese Studies being run in the Department of Chinese and Japanese Studies, University of Delhi, may not have materialised without the continuous support and encouragement provided by the Heads of the Department. Therefore, my sincere gratitude goes to all of them: particularly to Professor Kashi Ram Sharma and Dr. Brij Tankha.

The idea for giving an independent identity to the compilation of references on China and Japan as noted from Indian works in effect amounted to the attainment of objective of placing a kind of bibliographical control over available Indian publications on these important Area Studies streams which found strong and explicit backing and approbation from Dr. Manoranjan Mohanty (then Chief Editor, *China Report*) who volunteered to publish a part of the compilation in three issues of the *CR*. Therefore, I am immensely indebted to him for having provided the necessary encouragement and—if I may add—the primary opportunity to pursue this project rigorously so as to take it to its logical end. I have also to express my word of gratitude to Professor G.P. Deshpande for contributing a befitting Foreword to the document.

Further, I have to thank the members of staff and colleagues of libraries on the DU Campus (particularly Chinese and Japanese Studies Library and CRL), JNU Library, ICWA and ICSSR Libraries, and a number of other libraries in Delhi, for the help extended to my Assistants in making available the books and other sources needed by them for purposes of indexing. Thanks also go to a premier export house of books for substantial support provided by them in this regard.

Furthermore, a word of thanks goes to my team of typists and computer typists (HLS, NL, Robert Michael, etc.) who have done their job with a rare amount of dedication and competence and have produced a neat copy of a complicated text.

Finally and most importantly, I have to express my thanks to my dear publisher friend Praveen Mittal, for having unhesitatingly accepted this document for expeditious publication.

B.K. Kumar

USER'S GUIDE

The present bibliographic compendium purports to provide an integrated view of China and Japan. The entries, therefore, are unfolded through a subject-wise arrangement, which follows the Subject Schedule specifically devised for this issue (page xv).

Main Subjects appear in bold-face capital letters, and sub-subjects (sub-headings) are placed in bold-face capital and lower-case letters preceded in each case by a single dash. However, sub-subjects under appropriate sub-subjects are preceded by two dashes: to signify the constituent parts of the sub-groupings.

Each title is generally recorded only once, e.g., an item dealing with the theme of 'privatisation of economy' and 'economic reform measures' in China might be placed under the heading 'Economic Reforms' depending upon the emphasis of the article. In that case, the second theme/subject will be covered by an appropriate reference in the Subject Index.

BIBLIOGRAPHIC ENTRIES

Monographs

The entry element for a monograph may be the personal or corporate author, editor, compiler, or the title itself when the authorship is unidentifiable. The entry element is followed by the title and subtitle, place of publication, publisher's name, and year of publication.

Examples

(i) *Development for Whom?: A Report on the Chinese Development Strategies in Tibet and Their Impacts* (Dharamsala: Tibetan Youth Congress, Office of the Central Executive Committee, 1995).

(ii) Swamy, S.A., Trade and Industry in Japan: A Guide to Indian Entrepreneurs and Businessmen (New Delhi: Prentice-Hall of India, 1993).

Analytical Entries

Wherever relevant chapters or sections in composite volumes have been separately indexed, *which form constitutes a predominant part of this volume,* the elements of information are: the author's name, the title of the chapter/section followed by 'in' and the original name of the author if the author is the same, or the name of the author of the host monograph, the title and subtitle, which is followed within parentheses by place of publication, publisher's name, year of publication, and ends by specific page numbers covered.

Examples

(i) Hussain, Athar, 'Growth Patterns and Structural Changes in the Chinese Economy' in S.P.Gupta, et.al. (Eds.), *Development Patterns and Institutional Structures : China and India* (New Delhi : Allied Publishers, 1995), 18-44.

(ii) Saraswati, Baidynath, 'Rock Art of India and China: the Unity of Primal Vision' in Tan Chung (Ed.), *China and India* (New Delhi: Indian Council for Cultural Relations, 1994), 383-99.

Dissertations and Theses

The elements of information for the M.Phil. and Ph.D. Dissertations, which constitute a separate chapter, are as below.

First, the author's name, and the title and subtitle of the dissertation/thesis. Second, the name of the Department where the scholar was based, the name of the University, and the year of award of the degree. Third, MPT or PDT (explained in the chapter concerned).

Examples

(i) Chelli, Hari Kumar, *Chinese Communist Party's Policy Towards National Minorities: With Special Reference to Xinjiang* (New Delhi: Centre for East Asian Studies, JNU, 1990): MPT.

(ii) Yadav, Dinesh, *Sino-Pak Relations, 1960-1985* (Delhi: DCJS, DU, 1990): PDT.

SUBJECT INDEX

Though the Subject Schedule is fairly detailed for purposes of delineating the entries, a specific Subject Index which is largely a Key-Word Index, is appropriately placed at the end. It is hoped that it will serve as a supplementing and complementing medium of information to the main body of the bibliography.

AUTHOR INDEX

A personal name index is provided to facilitate access to the established authors/specialists in the field, joint authors, editors, translators, etc., concerned.

The numbers following each entry refer to the sequentially numbered citations in the main body of the bibliography.

A Note on Personal Names

There may be occasional differences in the spellings of the name of the same individual. No attempt could be made to standardize spellings. Chinese names are entered using whatever transliteration scheme is used on the title page or the contents page of the document (monograph). It is the policy of the Indexing Project to use the form of the author's name exactly as it is in the publication, with preference given to the form listed on the title page or in the contents of the publication.

SUBJECT SCHEDULE

SUPERCLASSES
- -Bibliography
- -Biography
- -Documents
- -History
- -Statistics
- -Study and Teaching

GENERAL AND MISCELLANEOUS
- -Bibliographies and Indexes
- -Chinese Studies
- -Japanese Studies

ANTHROPOLOGY AND SOCIOLOGY
- -Acculturation
- -Communal Relations
- -Community Development
- -Cross-cultural Contacts
- -Culture and Civilisation
- -Emigrants and Immigrants
- -Ethnic Groups
- -Folklore
- -Intellectuals
- -Inter-personal Relations
- -Migration
- -National Minorities
- -Physical Anthropology
- -Population
  - --Census
  - --Population Control
  - --Population Distribution
- -Race Relations
- -Rural Conditions
- -Social Change
- -Social Conditions
- -Social Customs
  - --Festivals
- -Social History
- -Social Problems
  - --Crime and Criminals
  - --Poverty
  - --Social Evils/Corruption
- -Social Sciences
  - --Sociology
- -Social Stratification
- -Social Structure
  - --Aged
  - --Caste
  - --Children
  - --Family and Marriage
  - --Women
  - --Youth
- -Social Work
  - --Social Welfare
- -Tradition and Traditionalism
- -Urban Studies

ARTS AND FINE ARTS
- -Architecture
- -Art, Buddhist
- -Art History
- -Calligraphy
- -Cinema
- -Dance
- -Decorative Art
- -Folk Arts
- -Iconography
- -Music
- -Paintings
- -Sculpture
  - --Cave Art
- -Theatre

-Prices and Pricing
System
-Private Sector
-Production System
-Public Sector
-Regional Economics
-Rural Development
-Special Economic Zones
(SEZs)
-Standard of Living
-Transportation And
Communication
-Urban Development

EDUCATION
-Administration
-Adult Education
-Distance Education
-Economic Aspects
-Educational History
-Educational Legislation
-Educational Philosophy
-Educational Situation
-Educational Sociology
-Elementary/School
Education
-Higher Education
-Literacy Situation
-Part-time Education
-Reforms And
Reorganisation
-Research And Testing
-Students
-Teachers And Teaching
-Technical/Professional
Education

GEOGRAPHY
-Historical Geography
-Political Geography
-Regional Geography
-Travel And Description

HISTORY
-Antiquities
-Archaeology And
Prehistory
-Chronology
-By Period : Ancient,
Medieval, Modern
-General History
-Historiography
-Local History
-Numismatics

INTERNATIONAL RELATIONS
-Foreign Policy: Parameters
and Principles
-Inter-governmental
Relations
:With CHINA And JAPAN
separately
-Africa
-Asia (East, South,
Southeast, West)
-Europe (East, West, etc.)
-ROC (Republic of
China)/Taiwan
-UN (United Nations)
-World
-World, Third

LANGUAGE
In Two Sections :
CHINESE And JAPANESE
-Comparative Linguistics
-Dialects
-Morphology And Syntax
-Phonology

CONTENTS

GENERAL AND MISCELLANEOUS

- CHINESE STUDIES

1 Cerr-Harris, Jill and Banerjee, Niloy (Eds.), *China Country Report* (New Delhi: South-South Solidarity, 1996).

2 Chopra, H.C., 'Manuscript Writing in Ancient China', in H.C. Chopra, *Oriental Manuscript Library: Origin, Development, Management and Conservation* (New Delhi: National Book Organisation, 1995), pp. 14-21.

3 Deshingkar, Giri, 'Chinese Studies in India: An Appraisal', in Tan Chung (Ed.), *China and India* (New Delhi: Indian Council for Cultural Relations, 1994), pp. 495-502; *Indian Horizons*, Special Issue, Vol. 43, Nos. 1-2, 1994.

4 Huang, I-shu, 'Pioneers and Cultural Bridges', in Tan Chung (Ed.), *China and India* (New Delhi: Indian Council for Cultural Relations, 1994), pp. 503-12; *Indian Horizons*, Special Issue, Vol. 43, Nos. 1-2, 1994.

- BIBLIOGRAPHIES AND INDEXES

5 Kumar, B.K., 'India's China Exploration: A Bibliographic Odyssey', in Tan Chung (Ed.), *China and India* (New Delhi: Indian Council for Cultural Relations, 1994), pp. 513-26; *Indian Horizons*, Special Issue, Vol. 43, Nos. 1-2, 1994.

- BIOGRAPHY

6 Puri, B.N., 'Prabodh Chandra Bagchi—A Sinologist', in B.N. Puri, *Ancient Indian Historiography: A Bi-Centenary Study* (Delhi: Atma Ram and Sons, 1994), pp. 272-74.

- EDUCATIONAL INSTITUTIONS

7 Geng, Yinzeng, 'History Revisited Here', in Tan Chung (Ed.), *China and India* (New Delhi: Indian Council for Cultural Relations, 1994), pp. 469-75; *Indian Horizons*, Special Issue, Vol. 43, Nos. 1-2, 1994.

- JAPANESE STUDIES

8 Chaudhuri, Sibadas (Ed.), India Internationalis Indicus, 8, 1992: Writings in Japanese Periodicals: Author

Catalogue: Cumulative List of Articles on Indological and Buddhistic Studies (With Key-Word Index Under Principal Subject Headings) pub. in Indian and Foreign Periodicals (Calcutta: Centre for Asian Documentation: Punthi-Pustak, 1995).

- TIBETAN STUDIES

9 Pathak, Suniti K. 'Modern Tibetan Studies in India', in Ashin Dasgupta, *et.al.* (Eds.), *M.M. Vidhusekhar Sastri Commemoration Volume* (Santiniketan: Research Publications, Visva-Bharati, 1990), Vol. 2, pp. 289-94.

ANTHROPOLOGY AND SOCIOLOGY

- ACCULTURATION

10 Ji, Xianlin, 'Endless Flow of Cross Cultural Currents Betweeen India and China', in Tan Chung (Ed.), *India and China* (New Delhi: Indian Council for Cultural Relations, 1994), pp. 5-10; *Indian Horizons*, Special Issue, Vol. 43, Nos. 1-2, 1994.

11 Jin, Dinghan, 'Give and Take in Sino-Indian Cultural Interface', in Tan Chung (Ed.), *India and China* (New Delhi: Indian Council for Cultural Relations, 1994), pp. 33-6; *Indian Horizons*, Special Issue, Vol. 43, Nos. 1-2, 1994.

12 Madan, T.N., 'Asia and the Modern West: Indian and Japanese Responses to Westernization', in T.N. Madan, *Pathways: Approaches to the Study of Society in India* (Delhi: Oxford University Press, 1994), pp. 226-45.

13 Mehrotra, Rachna, 'Cultural Influence Abroad: Central Asia and China', in Rachna Mehrotra, *Impact of Indian Culture on Nehru* (Delhi: Rahul Publishing House, 1996), pp. 130-38.

14 Pachow, W., 'Tan Yu-shan and Cultural Relations Between China and India', in Tan Chung (Ed.), *India and China* (New Delhi: Indian Council for Cultural Relations, 1994), pp. 183-92; *Indian Horizons*, Special Issue, Vol. 43, Nos. 1-2, 1994.

15 Tagore, Rabindranath, 'China and India', in Tan Chung (Ed.), *India and China* (New Delhi: Indian Council for

Cultural Relations, 1994), pp. 67-73; *Indian Horizons*, Special Issue, Vol. 43, Nos. 1-2, 1994.

16 Tan Chung, 'Ageless Brotherhood Between India and China', in Tan Chung (Ed.), *India and China* (New Delhi: Indian Council for Cultural Relations, 1994), pp. 11-31; *Indian Horizons*, Special Issue, Vol. 43, Nos. 1-2, 1994.

17 Tan Chung and Ray, Haraprasad 'Trans-Himalayan Multi-national Habitat', in Tan Chung (Ed.), *India and China* (New Delhi: Indian Council for Cultural Relations, 1994), pp. 291-312; *Indian Horizons*, Special Issue, Vol. 43, Nos. 1-2, 1994.

18 Tan, Yun-shan, 'The Chinese Hall: Cheena Bhavana', in Tan Chung (Ed.), *India and China* (New Delhi: Indian Council for Cultural Relations, 1994), pp. 177-81; *Indian Horizons*, Special Issue, Vol. 43, Nos. 1-2, 1994.

- CROSS-CULTURAL CONTACTS

19 Gandhi, Rajiv, 'Address of Prime Minister Rajiv Gandhi at Qinghua University, Beijing, on December 21, 1988', in Tan Chung (Ed.), *India and China* (New Delhi: Indian Council for Cultural Relations, 1994), pp. 529-43; *Indian Horizons*, Special Issue, Vol. 43, Nos. 1-2, 1994.

20 Ichimura, Shohei, 'The Sino-Indian Trans-Cultural Method of Madhyamika Dialectic: Nagarjuna to Seng-chao to Chi-ts'ang', in G. Kuppuram (Ed.), *Buddhist Heritage in India and Abroad* (Delhi: Sundeep Prakashan, 1992), pp. 239-66.

21 Jaspal Singh, 'India and China', in Jaspal Singh, *Society, Culture and Socio-Cultural Change* (New Delhi: National Book Organisation, 1996), pp. 116-19.

22 Narasimha Rao, P.V., 'Prime Minister Narasimha Rao's Address at Beijing University, on 9th September 1993', in Tan Chung (Ed.), *India and China* (New Delhi: Indian Council for Cultural Relations, 1994), pp. 545-55; *Indian Horizons*, Special Issue, Vol. 43, Nos. 1-2, 1994.

23 Shrivastava, P.S., 'Indian Culture in the Land of Snows', in M.C.P. Srivastava (Ed.), *Proceedings of the Seminar on Indian Culture Abroad* (Patna: Bihar Puravid Parishad, 1991), pp. 53-63.

24 Tagore, Rabindranath, 'Talks in China', in Rabindranath Tagore, *The English Writings of Rabindranath Tagore* (New Delhi: Sahitya Akademi, 1996), Vol. 2, pp. 571-686.

- CULTURE AND CIVILISATION

25 Choudhury, Paramesh, *North East, The Cradle of the Chinese Nation* (Calcutta: P. Choudhary, 1995).

26 Kao, Sefong and Tang, Shengming 'Residence Place and Self-esteem of Taiwan Aborigines', in Man Singh Das and Vijay Kumar Gupta (Eds.), *Transitional Development and Attitudinal Changes in Society* (New Delhi: M. D. Publications, 1996), pp. 19-28.

27 Kawachi, Yoshiko, 'Shakespeare and Japanese Culture', in Vikram Chopra (Ed.), *Shakespeare: Varied Perspectives* (Delhi: B.R. Publishing Corporation, 1996), pp. 65-78.

28 Ramjee Singh, 'Gandhiji's Letters to Chiang Kaishek and to Every Japanese', in Ramjee Singh, *Gandhi and the Twenty-First Century* (New Delhi: Peace Publishers, 1993), pp. 78-85.

29 Tagore, Rabindranath, 'On Oriental Culture and Japan's Mission', in Rabindranath Tagore, *The English Writings of Rabindranath Tagore;* ed. by Sisir Kumar Das (New Delhi: Sahitya Akademi, 1996), Vol. 3: A Miscellany, pp. 604-10.

30 Tagore, Rabindranath, 'The Spirit of Japan', in Rabindranath Tagore, *The English Writings of Rabindranath Tagore;* ed. by Sisir Kumar Das (New Delhi: Sahitya Akademi, 1996), Vol. 3: A Miscellany, pp. 364-75.

31 Tagore, Rabindranath, 'To the People of China', in Rabindranath Tagore, *The English Writings of Rabindranath Tagore;* ed. by Sisir Kumar Das (New Delhi: Sahitya Akademi, 1996), Vol. 3: A Miscellany, pp. 831-32.

32 Tagore, Rabindranath, 'Welcome to XuBeihong', in Rabindranath Tagore, *The English Writings of Rabindranath Tagore;* ed. by Sisir Kumar Das (New Delhi: Sahitya Akademi, 1996), Vol. 3: A Miscellany, pp. 850.

33 Tan, Yun-shan, 'Remembering Gurudeva's Affection for China', in Tan Chung (Ed.), *India and China* (New Delhi: Indian Council for Cultural Relations, 1994), pp. 193-95; *Indian Horizons*, Special Issue, Vol. 43, Nos. 1-2, 1994.

34 Wu, Baihui, 'My Tribute to Gurudeva', in Tan Chung (Ed.), *India and China* (New Delhi: Indian Council for Cultural Relations, 1994), pp. 109-10; *Indian Horizons*, Special Issue, Vol. 43, Nos. 1-2, 1994.

- EMIGRATION AND IMMIGRATION

35 Atkinson, Anne, 'Illegal Immigration: A Method of Acquiring Labour for Chinese Firms', in Jan Ryan (Ed.), *Chinese in Australia and New Zealand: A Multidisciplinary Approach* (New Delhi: New Age International, 1995), pp. 83-91.

36 Chan, H.D. Min-hsi, 'Community, Culture and Commerce: New Approaches to the History of Chinese in Australia', in Jan Ryan (Ed.), *Chinese in Australia and New Zealand: A Multidisciplinary Approach* (New Delhi: New Age International, 1995), pp. 106-07.

37 Fisher, Lynn, 'From Cultural Revolutionary Dancer to Sandgroper Choreographer: The Transformation of Susan Wang', in Jan Ryan (Ed.), *Chinese in Australia and New Zealand: A Multidisciplinary Approach* (New Delhi: New Age International, 1995), pp. 54-58

38 Giese, Diana, 'In the Presence of Living Beings—Many, In Fact, Dead: Struggling with Chinese Oral Histories', in Jan Ryan (Ed.), *Chinese in Australia and New Zealand: A Multidisciplinary Approach* (New Delhi: New Age International, 1995), pp. 35-44.

39 Jack, R. Ian, 'The Contribution of Archaeology to the History of the Overseas Chinese', in Jan Ryan (Ed.), *Chinese in Australia and New Zealand: A Multidisciplinary Approach* (New Delhi: New Age International, 1995), pp. 21-29.

40 Kim, Lee Su, 'Two Straits China Women Writers: Ruth Ho and Yeap Joo Kim', in A.L. Mcleod (Ed.), *Commonwealth and American Women's Discourse: Essays in Criticism* (New Delhi: Sterling Publishers, 1996), pp. 238-47.

41 Koi, Norma King, 'Discovering My Heritage: My Chinese Family History', in Jan Ryan (Ed.), *Chinese in Australia and New Zealand: A Multidisciplinary Approach* (New Delhi: New Age International, 1995), pp. 45-53.

42 Loh, Morag, 'Fighting Uphill: Australians of Chinese Descent in the Australian Defence Forms 1899-1951', in Jan Ryan (Ed.), *Chinese in Australia and New Zealand: A Multidisciplinary Approach* (New Delhi: New Age International, 1995), pp. 59-66.

43 Macgregor, Paul, 'Chinese: Australian? The Limits of Geography and Ethnicity as Determinants of Cultural Identity' in Jan Ryan (Ed.), *Chinese in Australia and New Zealand: A Multidisciplinary Approach* (New Delhi: New Age International, 1995), pp. 5-20.

44 Ng, James, 'Chinese Goldseekers in Otago, New Zealand', in Jan Ryan (Ed.), *Chinese in Australia and New Zealand: A Multidisciplinary Approach* (New Delhi: New Age International, 1995), pp. 30-34.

45 Norbu, Dawa, 'Tibetan Refugees in South Asia: A Case of Peaceful Adjustment', in S.D. Muni and Lok Raj Bara (Eds.), *Refugees and Regional Security in South Asia* (Delhi: Konark Publishers, 1996), pp. 151-55.

46 Presland, Gary, 'Detecting Chinese Crime in Nineteenth Century Victoria', in Jan Ryan (Ed.), *Chinese in Australia and New Zealand: A Multidisciplinary Approach* (New Delhi: New Age International, 1995), pp. 75-82.

47 Rankine, Wendy, 'Australia's Chinese Army Corps', in Jan Ryan (Ed.), *Chinese in Australia and New Zealand: A Multidisciplinary Approach* (New Delhi: New Age International, 1995), pp. 67-74.

48 Ryan, Jan, 'An Historical Approach to the Study of Morbidity and Mortality Amongst Chinese in Colonial Western Australia', in Jan Ryan (Ed.), *Chinese in Australia and New Zealand: A Multidisciplinary Approach* (New Delhi: New Age International, 1995), pp. 92-105.

49 Ryan, Jan (Ed.), *Chinese in Australia and New Zealand: A Multidisciplinary Approach* (New Delhi: New Age International, 1995).

- ETHNIC GROUPS

50 Hans, Asha, 'Tibetan Ethnicity and the China Policy of Assimilation', in K. Warikoo and Dawa Norbu (Eds.),

Ethnicity and Politics in Central Asia (New Delhi: South Asian Publishers, 1992), pp. 159-86.

51 Ramanathan, Indira, *China and the Ethnic Chinese in Malaysia and Indonesia*, 1949-1992 (New Delhi: Radiant Publishers, 1994).

52 *Tibetan Refugee Community Integrated Development Plan-II, 1995-2000* (Dharamsala: Planning Council, Central Tibetan Administration of His Holiness the Dalai Lama, 1994), 2 Vols.

- INTELLECTUALS

53 Subramaniam, V., 'Intellectuals in State, and Society in India and China: Some Critical Comparisons', in V. Subramaniam, *Political Theorizing in Asia: The Socio-Cultural Context* (Delhi: Ajanta Publications, 1994), pp. 1-19.

- NATIONAL MINORITIES

54 Choedon, Yeshi, 'China's National Minorities Policy: With Special Reference to Tibet', in K. Warikoo and Dawa Norbu (Eds.), *Ethnicity and Politics in Central Asia* (New Delhi: South Asian Publishers, 1992), pp. 187-203.

55 *Dharamsala: A Guide to Little Lahasa in India* (Dharamsala: Department of Information and International Relations, Central Tibetan Administration, 1996).

56 Long, Chun Liu and Wang, Jieru, 'Studies of Traditional Tea-Garden of Jinno Nationality, China', in S.K. Jain (Ed.), *Ethnobiology in Human Welfare: Proceedings of IV International Congress of Ethnobiology, Held at Lucknow, India, 1994* (New Delhi: Deep Publication, 1996), pp. 339-44.

57 Norbu, Dawa, 'China's Policy Towards National Minorities in 1990s', in K. Warikoo and Dawa Norbu, *Ethnicity and Politics in Central Asia* (New Delhi: South Asian Publishers, 1992), pp. 292-98.

58 Guan, Jian (Ed.), *Tai Minorities in China*, general editor, Sachchidanand Sahai (Gaya: Centre for South East Asian Studies, 1992-1993), 2 Vols. Vol. 1: *A Select Bibliography*; Vol. 2: *The Indigenous Religion and Theravada Buddhism in Ban Da Tui: A Dai Lue Village in Yunnan (China).*

- POPULATION PROBLEMS

59 Bose, Ashish, 'China: Basic Demographic Data, 1991', in Ashish Bose, *India and the Asian Population Perspective* (Delhi: B.R. Pub. Corporation, 1993), pp. 197-203.

60 Bose, Ashish, 'Population Perspective: India, China and the World', in S.R. Mohnot (Ed.), *Towards a New Global Order: Essays in Honour of Dr. L.M. Singhvi, in Recognition of His Service to Society* (New Delhi: Har-Anand Publications, 1993), pp. 263-71.

61 Bose, Ashish, 'Population Planning in China', in Ashish Bose, *India and the Asian Population Perspective* (Delhi: B.R. Pub. Corporation, 1993), pp. 19-24.

62 Hao, Hong Sheng, 'Mortality Levels, Trends and Differentials in China', in Kuttan Mahadevan (Ed.), *Differential Development and Demographic Dilemma: Perspectives from China and India* (Delhi: B.R. Pub. Corporation, 1994), pp. 225-50.

63 Tibetan Youth Congress, *Strangers in Their Own Country: Chinese Population Transfer in Tibet and its Impact: A Report* (Dharmsala: Tibetan Youth Congress, Office of the Central Executive Committee, 1994).

64 Sun, Te-Hsuing, 'Demographic Transition and Fertility Control Policies in Taiwan', in P. Krishnan, *et.al.* (Eds.), *Readings in Population Research: Policy, Methodology and Perspectives* (Delhi: B.R. Pub. Corporation, 1992), pp. 25-57.

65 Tuan, Chi-hsien, 'Demographic Characteristics of Population in China', in Kuttan Mahadevan (Ed.), *Differential Development and Demographic Dilemma: Perspectives from China and India* (Delhi: B.R. Pub. Corporation, 1994), pp. 151-62.

66 Tuan, Chi-Hsien, 'Ecology, Development and Population Regulation in China', in Kuttan Mahadevan (Ed.), *Differential Development and Demographic Dilemma: Perspectives from China and India* (Delhi: B.R. Pub. Corporation, 1994), pp. 57-125.

67 Tuan, Chi-hsien, 'Fertility of China', in Kuttan Mahadevan (Ed.), *Differential Development and*

Demographic Dilemma: Perspectives from China and India (Delhi: B.R. Pub. Corporation, 1994), pp. 163-202.

68 Tuan, Chi-hsien, 'Gender Selection and Fertility Regulation in the Process of Family Building in China', in P. Krishnan, *et.al.* (Eds.), *Readings in Population Research: Policy, Methodology and Perspectives* (Delhi: B.R. Pub. Corporation, 1992), pp. 403-72.

69 Tuan, Chi-hsien, 'Population and Development, the Challenge to China's Future', in Kuttan Mahadevan (Ed.), *Differential Development and Demographic Dilemma: Perspectives from China and India* (Delhi: B.R. Pub. Corporation, 1994), pp. 235-306.

70 Tuan, Chi-hsien, 'Population Control Policy in China', in Kuttan Mahadevan (Ed.), *Differential Development and Demographic Dilemma: Perspectives from China and India* (Delhi: B.R. Pub. Corporation, 1994), pp. 307-30.

71 Tuan, Chi-hsien, 'Population Planning and Management in China', in Kuttan Mahadevan (Ed.), *Differential Development and Demographic Dilemma: Perspectives from China and India* (Delhi: B.R. Pub. Corporation, 1994), pp. 37-48.

72 Yu, Jingyuan, 'Population Studies in China: 1970-1990', in P. Krishna, *et.al.* (Eds.), *Readings in Population Research: Policy, Methodology, and Perspectives* (Delhi: B.R. Pub. Corporation, 1992), pp. 375-401.

73 Yu, Jingyuan, 'Population Transition in China, 1950-1991', in Kuttan Mahadevan (Ed.), *Differential Development and Demographic Dilemma: Perspectives from China and India* (Delhi: B.R. Publication Corporation, 1994), pp. 395-404.

74 Yu, Jinguan, 'Systems Science Developed in China for the Study of Population Problems', in Kuttan Mahadevan and Parameshwara Krishnan (Eds.), *Methodology for Population Studies and Development* (New Delhi: Sage Publications, 1993), pp. 206-17.

- RURAL STUDIES

75 Aslam, M., 'Rural Transformation in People's Republic of China', in M. Aslam, *Integrated Rural Development in*

Asia: Concept, Practice and Perspective (New Delhi: Manohar, 1993), pp. 45-57 .

76 Mohanty, Manoranjan, 'In the Land of Rice and Fish: Researching Wuxi's Transformation', in Tan Chung (Ed.), *India and China* (New Delhi: Indian Council for Cultural Relations, 1994), pp. 279-89; *Indian Horizons*: Special Issue, Vol.43, Nos.1-2, 1994.

77 Chkama, Kunio and Kikuchi, Masao, 'Rural Infrastructure Development and Farmers' Participation: Farmers, Community and Local Government in Pre-War Japanese Village', in S. Hirashima and W. Gooneratne (Eds.), *State and Community in Local Resource Management: The Asian Experience* (New Delhi: Har-Anand Publications, 1996), pp. 41-3.

78 Ray, Samirendra N., 'Rural Development in Socialist Construction in Mao's China: An Analysis of Mao Zedong's Thought and Its Contemporary Relevance', in Girin Phukon and Dhiren Bhagawati (Eds.), *Mao Zedong and Social Reconstruction* (New Delhi: South Asian Publishers, 1996), pp. 85-96.

79 Zhang, Lubiao, 'Experiences and Perspectives of Eco-Villages in China', in M.S. Swaminathan (Ed.), *Ecotechnology and Rural Employment: A Dialogue* (Madras: Macmillan, 1994), pp. 165-68.

- SOCIAL DYNAMISM

80 Mahadevan, Kuttan, *et.al.*, *Society and Development in China and India* (Delhi: B.R. Pub. Corporation, 1994).

81 Masanori, Kikuchi. 'Social Transformation in the Soviet Union, China and Japan: A Comparative Study', in Manoranjan Mohanty (Ed.), *Chinese Revolution: Comparative Perspectives on Transformation of Non-Western Societies* (Delhi: Ajanta Publications, 1992), pp. 165-85.

82 Tims, Wouter. 'China: The Future of Reform', in Kanta Ahuja, *et.al.* (Eds.), *Regime Transformations and Global Realignments: Indo-European Dialogues on the Post-Cold War World* (New Delhi: Sage Publications, 1993), pp. 81-95.

83 Xing, Bensi. 'Certain Theoretical Issues Concerning Social Transformation in Contemporary China', in Manoranjan Mohanty (Ed.), *Chinese Revolution: Comparative Perspectives on Transformation of Non-Western Societies* (Delhi: Ajanta Publications, 1992), pp. 147-61.

- SOCIAL HISTORY

84 Dash, Narendra Kumar. 'Cultural Relations of India with Tibet and China', in B.U. Nayak and N.C. Ghosh (Eds.), *New Trends in Indian Art and Archaeology: S.R. Rao's 70th Birthday Felicitation Volume*, Vol. I (New Delhi: Aditya Prakashan, 1992), pp. 285-92.

85 Lokesh Chandra. 'The Cultural Heritage of Japan (in Japanese)', in Lokesh Chandra, *Cultural Heritage of India* (New Delhi: International Academy of Indian Culture; Aditya Prakashan, 1992), pp. 309-17.

86 Ray, Haraprasad. 'Indian Settlements in China—An Explanation of the Phenomena of Indian Diaspora From A.D. 1015 to 1487', in K.S. Mathur (Ed.), *Indian Ocean and Cultural Interaction, A.D. 1400-1800* (Pondicherry: Pondicherry University, 1996), pp. 52-81.

87 Ray, Haraprasad. 'An Inquiry into the Presence of the Chinese in South and Southeast Asia After the Voyages of Zheng He in Early Fifteenth Century', in K.S. Mathur (Ed.), *Mariners, Merchants and Oceans: Studies in Maritime History* (New Delhi: Manohar Publishers and Distributors, 1995), pp. 97-109.

88 Tan, Chung. 'Time in the Cultural Frame of China', in Kapila Vatsyayan (Ed.), *Concepts of Time: Ancient and Modern* (New Delhi: Indira Gandhi National Centre for the Arts, in association with Sterling Publishers, 1996), pp. 175-85 .

- SOCIAL INTERACTIONS

89 Narasimha Rao, P.V. 'Common Indo-China Approach for Asian Resurgence', in P.V. Narasimha Rao: *Selected Speeches* (New Delhi: Publications Division, Ministry of Information and Broadcasting, Government of India, 1995), Vol. 3, pp. 389-400; 'Speech at Beijing University, China, 9 September 1993'.

90 Prasad, Rajendra. 'Crown Prince Akihito's Visit' and 'Impressions of Japan', in Valmiki Choudhary (Ed.), *Dr. Rajendra Prasad: Correspondence and Select Documents* (New Delhi: Allied Publishers, 1995), Vol. 21, pp. 478-87.

- SOCIAL PROBLEMS

91 Fujimoto, Tetsuya. 'The Victimization Surveys for Child Abuse in Japan', in S.P. Singh Makkar and Paul C. Friday (Eds.), *Global Perspectives in Victimology* (Jalandhar: ABS Publications, 1993), pp. 70-90.

92 Prabhu, Shiraz. 'Poverty Alleviation and Role of Non-Government Organizations', in Carr-Harris, Jill, *China Country Report* (New Delhi: South-South Solidarity, 1996), pp. 29-39.

- SOCIAL SITUATION

93 Banerjee, Nashitish Chandra. 'A Comparison Between China and India', in Kashitish Chandra, *The Glimpses of Great Thoughts* (Calcutta: K.C. Banerjee, 1995), pp. 130-41.

- SOCIAL STRUCTURE

– The Aged

94 Bose, Ashish. 'The Aging Population of Japan', in Ashish Bose, *India and the Asian Population Perspective* (Delhi: B.R. Pub. Corporation, 1993), pp. 25-8.

95 Hermalin, Albert I. 'A Comparison of Alternative Approaches to Measuring Needs and Levels of Support Received Among the Elderly in Taiwan', in P. Krishnan, *et.al.* (Eds.), *Readings in Population Research: Policy, Methodology and Perspectives* (Delhi: B.R. Pub. Corporation, 1992), pp. 295-310.

96 Hirosima, Kiyoshi. 'The Living Arrangements and Familial Contacts of the Elderly in Japan', in P. Krishnan and K. Mahadevan (Eds.), *The Elderly Population in Developed and Developing World: Policies, Problems and Perspectives* (Delhi: B.R. Pub. Corporation, 1992), pp. 68-86.

97 Kalab, Kathleen A. 'Population and Family Characteristics of the Elderly in a Town in Northern

Japan', in P. Krishnan and K. Mahadevan (Eds.), *The Elderly Population in Developed and Developing World: Policies, Problems and Perspectives* (Delhi: B.R. Pub. Corporation, 1992), pp. 202-17.

98 Li, li. 'Subjecting Well-Being of Chinese Urban Elderly', in Man Singh Das and Vijay Kumar Gupta (Eds.), *Transitional Development and Attitudinal Changes in Society* (New Delhi: M.D. Publications, 1996), pp. 101-10.

99 Tuan, Chi-hsien. 'The Process of Population, Ageing and the Status of Old People in China', in P. Krishnan and K. Mahadevan (Eds.), *The Elderly Population in Developed and Developing World: Policies, Problems and Perspectives* (Delhi: B.R. Pub. Corporation, 1992), pp. 218-60.

100 Zhan, Zie. 'Population Aging and Economic Development in China', in P. Krishnan, *et.al.* (Eds.), *Readings in Population Research: Policy, Methodology and Perspectives* (Delhi: B.R. Pub. Corporation, 1992), pp. 373-81 .

– Family and Marriage

101 Abbot, Douglas A. 'An Evolving Redefinition of the Fatherhood Role in the People's Republic of China', in Man Singh Das and Vijay Kumar Gupta (Eds.), *Gender Roles and Family Analyses* (New Delhi: M.D. Publications, 1995), pp. 191-202.

102 Abbott, Douglas A. 'Married But Living Apart: Chinese Couples Seeking a Better Life', in Man Singh Das and Vijay Kumar Gupta (Eds.), *Gender Roles and Family Analyses* (New Delhi: M.D. Publications, 1995), pp. 61-71.

103 Chung, Byung-Ho. 'Labor-Market Demand for Working Mothers and the Evolution of Day Care System in Japan', in Man Singh Das and Vijay Kumar Gupta (Eds.), *Gender Roles and Family Analyses* (New Delhi: M.D. Publications, 1995), pp. 119-37.

104 Crook, John. 'Explaining Tibetan Polyandry: Socio-Cultural, Demographic and Biological Perspectives', in John Crook, *Himalayan Buddhist Villages: Environment,*

Resources, Society and Religious Life in Zangskar, Ladakh (Delhi: Motilal Banarasidas, 1994), pp. 735-86.

105 Wang, Rusong, *et.al.* 'Family Transition and Its Human Ecological Implications in China', in Napoleon Wolanski and Barry Bogin (Eds.), *The Family As An Environment of Human Development* (Delhi: Kamla Raj Enterprises, 1996), pp. 101-11.

106 Wolanski, Napoleon. 'The Family and Child Growth (Cross-Cultural Studies in Poland, Japan, South Korea and Mexico)', in Napoleon Wolanski and Barry Bogin (Eds.), *The Family As An Environment of Human Development* (Delhi: Kamla Raj Enterprises, 1996), pp. 185-99.

-- Women

107 Chakrabarti, Shrimati. 'Health and Status of Women', in Jill Carr-Harris and Niloy Banerjee (Eds.), *China Country Report* (New Delhi: South-South Solidarity, 1996), pp. 40-55.

108 Cheung, Fanny M. 'Promoting Women's Development in Hong Kong', in Committee on Women's Studies in Asia (Ed.), *Women's Studies, Women's Lives, Theory and Practice in South and Southeast Asia* (New Delhi: Kali for Women, 1994), pp. 59-73.

109 Chi, Peng. 'Chinese Women After the Cultural Revolution', in Maithili Vishwanathan (Ed.), *Country Experience in Women and Work* (Jaipur: Printwell, 1994), pp. 108-67.

110 Ghosh, S.K. 'China' in S.K. Ghosh, *The World of Prostitutes* (New Delhi: APH Pub. Corporation, 1996), pp. 91-93.

111 Ghosh, S.K. 'Japan' in S.K. Ghosh, *The World of Prostitutes* (New Delhi: APH Pub. Corporation, 1996), pp. 271-74.

112 Kato, Ryoko. 'Japanese Women: Subordination or Domination' in Man Singh Das and Vijay Kumar Gupta (Eds.), *Women and Her Environment* (New Delhi: M.D. Publications, 1995), pp. 147-52.

113 Kelkar, Govind. *Women and the Land Question in China* (New Delhi: Nehru Memorial Museum and Library, 1990). (Occasional Papers on History and Society, Second Series, 30).

114 Li, Xiaojiang. 'My Path to Womanhood' in Committee on Women's Studies in Asia (Ed.), *Women's Studies, Women's Lives, Theory and Practice in South and Southeast Asia* (New Delhi: Kali for Women, 1994), pp. 100-12 .

115 Liang, Jun. 'A Serious Mission', in Committee on Women's Studies in Asia (Ed.), *Women's Studies, Women's Lives, Theory and Practice in South and Southeast Asia* (New Delhi: Kali for Women, 1994), pp. 114-22.

116 Mohanty, Manoranjan. *Women's Status in China (1980s-1990s)* (New Delhi: South-South Solidarity, 1990).

117 Muramatsu, Yasuko. 'An Exploratory Journey', in Committee on Women's Studies in Asia (Ed.), *Women's Studies, Women's Lives, Theory and Practice in South and Southeast Asia* (New Delhi: Kali for Women, 1994), pp. 196-208.

118 2nd ICA/Japan Training Course for Rural Women Leaders of Agricultural Cooperatives in Asia, 1992: A Report (New Delhi: International Cooperative Alliance, Regional Office for Asia and the Pacific, 1993).

119 Sharma, Manish. 'China: The Law File (and) a Critical Survey', in Manish Sharma, *When Fathers Rape: A Socio-Psychological-Global Study* (New Delhi: APH Pub. Corporation, 1996), pp. 254-61.

119A Tibetan Women: *Oppression and Discrimination in Occupied-Tibet: National Report on Tibetan Women* (Dharamsala: Central Tibetan Administration, 1995).

120 Tuan, Chi-hsien. 'Marital Status of Chinese Women', in Kuttan Mahadevan (Ed.), *Differential Development and Demographic Dilemma: Perspectives From China and India* (Delhi: B.R. Pub. Corporation, 1994), pp. 67-100.

121 Tuan, Chi-hsien. 'Status of Women and Family Planning: Perspectives from China', in Kuttan Mahadevan (Ed.), *Differential Development and Demographic Dilemma:*

Perspectives From China and India (Delhi: B.R. Pub. Corporation, 1994), pp. 363-76.

122 Yamashita, Akiko. 'Women's Issues in Japan', in T. Dayanandan Francis and F.J. Balasundaram (Eds.), *Asian Expressions of Christian Commitment: A Reader in Asian Theology* (Madras: Christian Literature Society, 1992), pp. 231-37.

-- Youth

123 Huang, Zhi-Jian. 'Ten Years' Reform of China and the Great Changes of the Youth Value System', in Y.C. Simhadri (Ed.), *Global Youth, Peace and Development: The Role of Science and Technology in Contemporary Society* (Delhi: Ajanta Publications, 1991), Vol. 1, pp. 549-54.

- URBAN STUDIES

124 Postow, Dudley L. 'The Giant Cities of China: Patterns of Dominance and Integration', in Bernd Hamm (Ed.), *Progress in Social Ecology* (New Delhi: Mittal Publications, 1992), pp. 135-51.

125 Zhao, Ziaohua. 'Urbanization and Migration in China', in Kuttan Mahadevan (Ed.), *Differential Development and Demographic Dilemma: Perspectives From China and India* (Delhi: B.R. Pub. Corporation, 1994), pp. 307-34.

ARTS AND FINE ARTS

- ARCHITECTURE

126 Denwood, Philip. 'Tibetan Architecture', in Pratapaditya Pillai (Ed.), *On the Path to Void: Buddhist Art of the Tibetan Realm* (Mumbai: Marg Publications, 1996), pp. 46-65.

127 Dorjee, Pema. *Stupa and Its Technology: A Tibeto-Buddhist Perspective* (New Delhi: Indira Gandhi Centre for the Arts and Motilal Banarasidas Publishers, 1996).

128 Goepper, Roger. 'Early Buddhist Architecture in Alchi' in Pratapaditya Pillai (Ed.), *On the Path to Void: Buddhist Art of the Tibetan Realm* (Mumbai: Marg Publications, 1996), pp. 82-99 .

129 Krishna Murthy, K. 'Buddhist Art and Architecture of Japan', in K. Krishna Murthy, *Studies in Buddhism* (Delhi: Sundeep Prakashan, 1996), pp. 217-22.

130 Lo Bue, Erberto F. 'The Sacred Enclave of Gyantse', in Pratapaditya Pillai (Ed.), *On the Path to Void: Buddhist Art of the Tibetan Realm* (Mumbai: Marg Publications, 1996), pp. 122-41.

131 Pritzker, Thomas J. 'Tabo Monastery: The Sacred Precinct', in Pratapaditya Pillai (Ed.), *On the Path to Void: Buddhist Art of the Tibetan Realm* (Mumbai: Marg Publications, 1996), pp. 66-81.

132 Singer, Jane Casey. 'Early Thankas: Eleventh-Thirteenth Centuries', in Pratapaditya Pillai (Ed.), *On the Path to Void: Buddhist Art of the Tibetan Realm* (Mumbai: Marg Publications, 1996), pp. 180-95.

- ART HISTORY

133 Banerjee, P. 'The Spread of Indian Art and Culture to Central Asia and China', in Tan Chung (Ed.), *China and India* (New Delhi: Council for Cultural Relations, 1994), pp. 365-81; *Indian Horizons*, Special Issue, Vol. 43, Nos. 1-2, 1994.

134 Berger, G.A. 'Conservation of Tibetan Thangka', in G.A. Berger, *Recent Trends in Conservation of Art Heritage: Dr. O.P. Agrawal Felicitation Volume* (Delhi: Agam Kala Prakashan, 1996), pp. 215-22.

135 Koki, Yamagishi. 'Some Evidences of Indian Influence on Japanese Ancient Arts', in Kalpakam Sankarnarayan, *et.al.* (Eds.), *Buddhism in India and Abroad: An Integrating Influence in Vedic and Post-Vedic Perspective* (Mumbai: Somaiya Publications, 1996), pp. 296-300.

136 Krishna Murthy, K. 'The Buddhist Art Tradition of China', in K. Krishna Murthy, *Studies in Buddhism* (Delhi: Sundeep Prakashan, 1996), pp. 213-16.

137 Lokesh Chandra. *Transcendental Art of Tibet* (New Delhi: International Academy of Indian Culture:Aditya Prakashan, 1996).

138 Mackeraras, Colin. 'The Rise of Chinese Regional Theatre During the Ming Dynasty (1364-1644)', in

Arvind Sharma (Ed.), *Perspectives on History and Culture: Essays in Honour of Professor D.P. Singhal (1925-1986)*, A Memorial Volume (Delhi: Sri Satguru Publications, 1992), pp. 91-105.

139 Pratapaditya Pal (Ed.), *On the Path to Void: Buddhist Art of the Tibetan Realm* (Mumbai: Marg Publications, 1996).

140 Saraswati, Baidyanath. 'Rock Art of India and China: The Unity of Primal Vision', in Tan Chung (Ed.), *China and India* (New Delhi: Indian Council for Cultural Relations, 1994), pp. 383-99; *Indian Horizons*, Special Issue, Vol. 43, Nos. 1-2, 1994.

- ART INSTITUTIONS

141 Chandrasekharan, Bagyalakshmi. 'Sister Institutions: IGNCA and Dunhuang Academy', in Tan Chung (Ed.), *China and India* (New Delhi: Indian Council for Cultural Relations, 1994), pp. 401-07; *Indian Horizons*, Special Issue, Vol. 43, Nos. 1-2, 1994.

- DANCES

142 Sakakibara, Kiitsu. 'Dances of China', in Kiitsu Sakakibara, *Dances of Asia* (Chandigarh: Abhishek Publications, 1992), pp. 139-87.

143 Sakakibara, Kiitsu. 'Dances of Japan', in Kiitsu Sakakibara, *Dances of Asia* (Chandigarh: Abhishek Publications, 1992), pp. 188-213.

144 Sakakibara, Kiitsu. 'Dances of Tibet', in Kiitsu Sakakibara, *Dances of Asia* (Chandigarh: Abhishek Publications, 1992), pp. 117-21.

- FOLK OPERA

145 Josayma, Cynthia Bridgman, *et.al. Drowa Sangmo: Tibetan Folk Opera* (Dharamsala: Library of Tibetan Works and Archives, 1990).

146 Ross, Joanna. *Lhamo: Opera From the Roof of the World* (New Delhi: Paljor Publications, 1995).

- ICONOGRAPHY

147 Bartholomew, Terese Tse. 'Spirit King, Demon, and God of Wealth, Ganesh, in East Asia', in Pratapaditya Pal

(Ed.), *Ganesh: The Benevolent* (Bombay: Marg Publications, 1995), pp. 115-32.

- MUSIC

148 Durga, S.A.K. 'Western Influence Upon the Musics of Japan, China, India and Indonesia', in S.A.K. Durga, *Ethnomusicology: A Study of Intercultural Musicology* (Madras: Center for Ethnomusicology, 1996), pp. 42-54.

149 Pian, Rulan Chao. 'Text Setting and the Use of Tune Types in Chinese Dramatic and Narrative Music', in Bonnie C. Wade (Ed.), *Text, Tone and Tune: Parameter of Music in Multicultural Perspective* (New Delhi: American Institute of Indian Studies and Oxford, IBH, 1993), pp. 201-33.

150 Watanabe, Mamoru. 'European Music in Japan', in O.P. Joshi, *Sociology of Oriental Music: A Reader* (Jaipur: Illustrated Book Publishers, 1992), pp. 295-307.

- PAINTINGS

151 Bhattacharya, A.K. 'Chinese Paintings—A Study in Its History', in Shyamalkanti Chakravarti (Ed.), *Vinayatoshini: Benoytosh Centenary Volume* (Naihiti, West Bengal: Benoytosh Centenary Committee, 1996), pp. 90-95.

152 Henss, Michael. 'Wall-Paintings in Western Tibet', in Pratapaditya Pillai (Ed.), *On the Path to Void: Buddhist Art of the Tibetan Realm* (Mumbai: Marg Publications, 1996), pp. 196-225.

153 Mukhopadhyay, Amit. 'China', in Amit Mukhopadhyay, *VIII Triennale India, 17 February—15 March 1994, Venue, Rabindra Bhavan Galleries, National Gallery of Art, All India Fine Arts and Crafts Society* (New Delhi: Lalit Kala Akademi, 1994), pp. 25-28.

154 Mukhopadhyay, Amit. 'Japan', in Amit Mukhopadhyay, *VIII Triennale India, 17 February—15 March 1994, Venue, Rabindra Bhavan Galleries, National Gallery of Art, All India Fine Arts and Crafts Society* (New Delhi: Lalit Kala Akademi, 1994), pp. 48-49.

155 Reynolds, Valrae. 'Fabric Images and Their Special Role in Tibet', in Pratapaditya Pillai (Ed.), *On the Path to Void:*

Buddhist Art of the Tibetan Realm (Mumbai: Marg Publications, 1996), pp. 244-57.

156 Wanzhang, Ge. 'Learning to Paint Thankas', in Pratapaditya Pillai (Ed.), *On the Path to Void: Buddhist Art of the Tibetan Realm* (Mumbai: Marg Publications, 1996), pp. 258-69.

- SCULPTURE

157 Bills, Sheih C. 'Sino-Tibetan Sculpture: The Tibetan Legacy', in Pratapaditya Pillai (Ed.), *On the Path to Void: Buddhist Art of the Tibetan Realm* (Mumbai: Marg Publications, 1996), pp. 142-61.

158 Blyth-Hill, Victoria. 'The Conservation of Thankas', in Pratapaditya Pillai (Ed.), *On the Path to Void: Buddhist Art of the Tibetan Realm* (Mumbai: Marg Publications, 1996), pp. 270-81.

159 Chen, Zao Fu. 'Discovery of Rock Art in China', in Michel Lorblanchet (Ed.), *Rock Art in the Old World: Papers Presented in Symposium A of the AURA Congress, Darwin, Australia, 1988* (New Delhi: Indira Gandhi National Centre for the Arts, 1992), pp. 371-81.

160 Chen, Zao Fu. 'Praying Figures in the Zuojiang River Valley', in Michel Lorblanchet (Ed.), *Rock Art in the Old World: Papers Presented in Symposium A of the AURA Congress, Darwin, Australia, 1988* (New Delhi: Indira Gandhi National Centre for the Arts, 1992), pp. 361-71.

161 Duan, Wenjie. *Dunhuang Art: Through the Eyes of Duan Wenjie*, edited and introduced by Tan Chung (New Delhi: Indira Gandhi National Centre for the Arts; Abhinav Publications, 1994).

162 Fisher, Robert. 'Early Chinese Jadges', in Stephen Markel (Ed.), *The World of Jade* (Bombay: Marg Publications, 1992), pp. 9-20.

163 Goepper, Roger. 'Murals in the Early Temples of Alchi', in Pratapaditya Pillai (Ed.), *On the Path to Void: Buddhist Art of the Tibetan Realm* (Mumbai: Marg Publications, 1996), pp. 226-43.

164 Gorakshkar, Sadashiv. 'Metal Sculptures of Western Tibet: A Consideration of Style During the Period of Rin-

Chen-Bzang-Po', in L.K. Srinivasan, *et.al.* (Eds.), *Sri Nagabhinandanam: Dr. M.S. Nagaraja Rao Festschrift: Eassya on Art, Culture, History, Archaeology, Epigraphy and Conservation of Cultural Property of India and Neighbouring Countries* (Bangalore: Dr. M.S. Nagaraja Rao Felicitation Committee, 1995), Vol. 1, pp. 325-34.

165 Henss, Michael. 'Early Tibetan Sculpture', in Pratapaditya Pillai (Ed.), *On the Path to Void: Buddhist Art of the Tibetan Realm* (Mumbai: Marg Publications, 1996), pp. 100-21.

166 Reddy, Chandra L. 'Tibetan Bronzes: Technical Observations', in Pratapaditya Pillai (Ed.), *On the Path to Void: Buddhist Art of the Tibetan Realm* (Mumbai: Marg Publications, 1996), pp. 162-79.

167 Krishna Murthy, K. 'The Buddhist Art Tradition of China', in G. Kuppuram (Ed.), *Buddhist Heritage in India and Abroad* (Delhi: Sundeep Prakashan, 1992), pp. 75-77.

168 Tan, Chung. 'Introducing Dunhuang Cave Art', in Kewal Krishan Mittal and Ashivini Agrawal (Eds.), *Buddhist Art and Thought* (New Delhi: Harman Publishing House, 1993), pp. 81-7.

169 Vatsyayan, Kapila. India Calling Dunhuang', in Tan Chung (Ed.), *China and India* (New Delhi: Indian Council for Cultural Relations, 1994), pp. 357-64; *Indian Horizons*, Vol. 43, Nos. 1-2, 1994.

170 Watt, James C.Y. 'The Working of Jade in the Ming and Qing Dynasties', in Stephen Markel (Ed.), *The World of Jade* (Bombay: Marg Publications, 1992), pp. 21-34.

171 Krishna Murthy, K. 'The Tibetan Astral Iconography', in K. Krishna Murthy, *Studies in Buddhism* (Delhi: Sundeep Prakashan, 1996), pp. 199-204.

COMMUNICATIONS AND MEDIA

- RADIO AND TELEVISION

172 Lo, Terence. 'No News is Bad News: 4 June and Individualism in Hong Kong', in David French and Michael Richards (Eds.), *Contemporary Television: Eastern*

Perspectives (New Delhi: Sage Publications, 1996), pp. 321-39.

173 Lo, Terence and Ng, Chung-Bong. 'The Evolution of Prime-Time Television Scheduling in Hong Kong', in David French and Michael Richards (Eds.), *Contemporary Television: Eastern Perspectives* (New Delhi: Sage Publications, 1996), pp. 200-20.

BOOKS AND BOOK PUBLISHING

174 Comber, Leon. 'The Chinese Book World Before and After Tiananmen Square', in Narendra Kumar (Ed.), *Afro-Asian Publishing: Contemporary Trends* (New Delhi: Institute of Book Pub., 1992), pp. 111-24.

175 Minowa, Shiglo. 'Publishing in Japan', in Narendra Kumar (Ed.), *Afro-Asian Publishing: Contemporary Trends* (New Delhi: Institute of Book Pub., 1992), pp. 141-56.

176 Ng, Alex. 'Village Life Collections in the New Territories of Hong Kong', in C.P. Vashishth (Ed.), *Libraries as Rural Community Resource Centres: Papers and Proceedings of the Workshop on Rural Community Resource Centres, New Delhi, 1992* (Delhi: B.R. Pub. Corporation, 1995), pp. 200-10.

177 Wu, Yishan, *et.al.* 'Bibliometric Studies in China and ISTIC's Approach', in I.K. Ravichandra Rao (Ed.), *Papers Presented for Third International Conference on Informatics, August 1991, Bangalore: Informatics-91* (Bangalore: DRTC, 1992), pp. 1-22.

COOKERY

178 Bubber, Purobi. The Flavours of China: Over 300 Authentic Vegetarian and Non-Vegetarian Chinese Recipes Free of Ajinomoto (Bombay: Vakils, Feffer and Simons, 1995).

DEFENCE AND STRATEGY

- ARMY/ARMY SERVICE

179 Baranwal, Jayant. 'The People's Liberation Army', in Jayant Baranwal (Ed.), *Military Yearbook, 1991-92* (New Delhi: Guide Publications, 1991), pp. 313-90.

180 Baranwal, Jayant. 'The People's Liberation Army', in Jayant Baranwal (Ed.), *Military Yearbook, 1991-92* (New Delhi: Guide Publications, 1993), pp. 191-95.

- DEFENCE POLICY

181 Acharya, Alka. 'Japan's Defence Capability in Transition', in Jasjit Singh (Ed.), *Asian Strategic Review, 1991-92* (Delhi: Institute for Defence Studies and Analyses, 1992), pp. 324-39.

182 Baranwal, Jayant. 'Japan—Self-Defence Forces', in Jayant Barawal, *SP's Military Yearbook, 1996* (New Delhi: Guide Publications, 1996), pp. 29-42.

183 Fukiharu, Toshitaka. 'Tripolar World and the Strategies for Japan: A Cost-Benefit Analysis', in Manas Chatterji, *et.al.* (Eds.), *Arms Spending, Development and Security* (New Delhi: APH Pub. Corporation, 1996), pp. 293-300.

184 Ishida, Takeshi. 'Nonviolent Strategies for Conflict Resolution in the Post-Cold War Environment: A View From Japan', in Mahendra Kumar (Ed.), *Legacy and Future of Nonviolence* (New Delhi: Gandhi Peace Foundation, 1996), pp. 240-44.

185 Malhotra, Sanjana. 'Japanese Defence in the 1990s', in Jasjit Singh (Ed.), *Asian Strategic Review, 1993-94* (New Delhi: Institute for Defence Studies and Analyses, 1994), pp. 294-305.

186 Swaran Singh. 'China's Defence Production', in Jasjit Singh (Ed.), *Asian Strategic Review, 1993-94* (New Delhi: Institute for Defence Studies and Analyses, 1994), pp. 256-94.

187 Baranwal, Jayant. 'Japan', in Jayant Baranwal (Ed.), *SP's Military Yearbook, 1995* (New Delhi: Guide Publications, 1995), pp. 225-26.

188 Bhagat, P.S. 'The Chinese Mind: What Will China Do Next', in Thomas Mathew, *Lt. Gen. P.S. Bhagat, PVSM, VC: A Biography* (New Delhi: Lancer International, 1994), pp. 497-505.

189 Baranwal, Jayant. 'China', in Jayant Baranwal (Ed.), *SP's Military Yearbook, 1995* (New Delhi: Guide Publications, 1995), pp. 221-23.

- MILITARY AFFAIRS

190 Deshingkar, Giri. 'Mao Zedong's Military Thought: A Perspective', in Girin Phukon and Dhiren Bhagawati (Eds.), *Mao Zedong and Social Reconstruction* (New Delhi: South Asian Publishers, 1996), pp. 142-48.

191 Dutta, Sujit. 'China's Military System', in Jasjit Singh (Ed.), *Asian Strategic Review, 1991-92* (New Delhi: Institute for Defence Studies and Analyses, 1992), pp. 227-85.

- MILITARY HARDWARE

192 Narayan, Rajiv. 'Missiles of China, Pakistan and India', in Rajiv Narayan, *Indo-Pak Relations: Viewpoints, 1989-1996* (New Delhi: Lancer Publishers, 1996), pp. 181-85.

193 Swaran Singh. 'Sino-Russian Techno-Military Cooperation', in Jasjit Singh (Ed.), *Asian Strategic Review, 1995-96* (New Delhi: Institute for Defence Studies and Analyses, 1996), pp. 174-97.

194. Swaran Singh. 'China's Military Modernization', in Jasjit Singh (Ed.), *Asian Strategic Review, 1993-94* (New Delhi: Institute for Defence Studies and Analyses, 1994), pp. 297-305.

- NUCLEAR ARMAMENT/POLICY

195 Chopra, V.D. *Nuclear Ambitions of Japan* (New Delhi: Gyan Publishing House, 1995).

196 Kapur, K.D. 'China and the Korean Nuclear Crisis', in K.D. Kapur, *Nuclear Diplomacy in East Asia: U.S. and the Korean Nuclear Crisis Management* (New Delhi: Lancers Books, 1995), pp. 302-08.

197 Kapur, K.D. 'Nuclear Policy of Japan and the Korean Nuclear Crisis', in K.D. Kapur, *Nuclear Diplomacy in East Asia: U.S. and the Korean Nuclear Crisis Management* (New Delhi: Lancers Books, 1995), pp. 329-65.

198 Lung, Trini. 'Nuclear Power Development and People's Movements in East Asia', in Sunderlal Bahuguna, *et.al.* (Eds.), *Environment Crisis and Sustainable Development* (Dehra Dun: Natraj Publishers, 1992), pp. 338-49.

199 Nair, V.K. 'China: The Threat', in V.K. Nair, *Nuclear India* (New Delhi: Lancer International, 1992), pp. 29-47.

200 Pollack, Jonathan D. 'China and Asia's Nuclear Defence', in Francine R. Frankel (Ed.), *Bridging the Non-Proliferation Divide: The United States and India* (Delhi: Konark Publishers, 1995), pp. 112-37.

201 Shyam Babu, D. 'China's Nuclear U-turn' in D. Shyam Babu, *Nuclear Non—Proliferation: Towards a Universal NPT Regime* (Delhi: Konark Publishers, 1992), pp. 119-31.

202 Sundarji, K. (Krishnaswami). 'Nuclear Threat From China and Others', in K. Sunderji, *Blind Men of Hindoostan: Indo-Pak Nuclear War* (New Delhi: UBS Publishers' Distributors, 1993), pp. 141-57.

- STRATEGIC AND SECURITY PERCEPTION

203 Banerjee, D. 'Sino-Indian Strategic Relations: From Stability to Cooperation', in Tan Chung (Ed.), *China and India* (New Delhi: Indian Council for Cultural Relations, 1994), pp. 329-41; *Indian Horizons*, Special Issue, Vol. 43, Nos. 1-2, 1994.

204 Chellaney, Brahma. 'Regional Security Implications of the Diffusion of Advanced Weapons and Technologies to China, India and Pakistan' in V.A. Pai Panandiker (Ed.), *India's Policy Problems* (Delhi: Konark Publishers, 1996), Vol. 2, pp. 3-51.

205 Cordonnier, Isabelle. 'China: A Proliferating Agent', in Dipankar Banerjee (Ed.), *Security in the New World Order: An Indo-French Dialogue* (New Delhi: Institute for Defence Studies and Analyses, 1994), pp. 191-7.

206 Joshi, Sanjana. 'East Asian Security Environment', in Jasjit Singh (Ed.), *Asian Strategic Review, 1994-95* (New Delhi: Institute for Defence Studies and Analyses, 1995), pp. 295-310.

206A Song, Xiesong and Dong, Weibo. 'The Occurrence and Control of Diseases, Insects, Weeds, and Rodents of Groundnut in China', in C.L.L. Gowda, *et.al.* (Eds.), *Achieving High Groundnut Yields: Proceedings of an International Workshop, August 1995, Shandong Peanut*

Research Institute (SPRI), Laixi, Shandong, China (Patancheru: ICRISAT, 1996), pp. 233-38.

ECONOMY

- AGRICULTURAL SITUATION

-- Agro-Based Industries

207 Banerjee, Niloy. 'Agriculture and Rural Industries', in Jill Carr-Harris and Niloy Benerjee (Eds.), *China Country Report* (New Delhi: South-South Solidarity, 1996), pp. 11-28.

208 Liu, Zhaoguang. 'A Local Resource-Centred Approach to Rural Transformation: Agro-based Cottage Industries in Western Sichuan, China', in N.S. Jodha, *et.al., Sustainable Mountain in Agriculture* (New Delhi: Oxford and IBH Publishing Company, 1992), Vol. 2, pp. 637-50.

- AGRO-FORESTRY

209 Li, Bo. 'Sustainable Development of Pasture Industry in China', in Panjab Singh, *et.al.* (Eds.), *Agroforestry Systems for Sustainable Land Use* (New Delhi: Oxford and IBH Publishing Company, 1994), pp. 192-203.

210 Negi, S.S. 'China', in S.S. Negi, *Forestry Research in Tropical Asia-Pacific* (New Delhi: M.D. Publications, 1995), pp. 59-65.

211 Negi, S.S. 'Japan', in S.S. Negi, *Forestry Research in Tropical Asia-Pacific* (New Delhi: M.D. Publications, 1995), pp. 119-26.

212 Zhu, Zhao Hu. 'Agroforestry in China—An Overview', in P.K. Khosla and D.K. Khurana (Eds.), *Agroforestry For Rural Needs: Workshop Proceedings* (Solan: Indian Society of Tree Scientists, 1993), Vol. 2, pp. 378-88.

-- Cooperatives

213 Guo, Yong Kang. *Perspective and Project Planning for Agricultural Cooperative Sector in China (Gansu Province): Report of the ICA Study Mission* (New Delhi: International Cooperative Alliance, Regional Office for Asia and the Pacific, 1991).

214 Guo, Yong Kang. *ICA/JA ZENCHU/IDACA Regional Seminar on Perspective Planning for Regional Development by Agricultural Cooperatives, Tokyo (Japan), 8-26 November 1993: A Report* (New Delhi: International Cooperative Alliance, Regional Office for Asia and the Pacific, 1994).

215 'Japanese Situation of Women's Association of Agricultural Cooperatives and the Future Prospects', in Daman Prakash (Comp.), *Report of the Third ICA/Japan Training Course for Rural Women Leaders of Agricultural Cooperatives in Asia, 1993* (New Delhi: International Cooperative Alliance, Regional Offices for Asia and the Pacific, 1993), pp. 35-42.

216 'National Situation Paper—China', in G.C. Shrotriya and Daman Prakash (Eds.), *Environment and Sustainable Cooperative Development: An Asian Regional Study* (New Delhi: International Cooperative Alliance, Regional Office for Asia and the Pacific, 1992), pp. 53-62.

217 'National Situation Paper—Japan', in G.C. Shrotriya and Daman Prakash (Eds.), *Environment and Sustainable Cooperative Development: An Asian Regional Study* (New Delhi: International Cooperative Alliance, Regional Office for Asia and the Pacific, 1992), pp. 138-68.

-- Crop Production

218 Chen. Yue. 'Sorghum Research in China', in Asian Sorghum Researchers' Consultative Meeting, *Collaborative Sorghum Research in Asia* (Patancheru, A.P.: ICRISAT, 1993), pp. 29-33.

219 'China', *in Teatech, 1993: Proceedings of the International Symposium on Tea Science and Human Health, January 11-14, 1993, Calcutta* (Calcutta: Tea Research Association, 1993), pp. 22-30.

220. Goto, Tadasi. 'Application of Near Infrared Spectroscopy for Quality Evaluation and Process Control on Japanese Green Tea', in *Teatech, 1993: Proceedings of the International Symposium on Tea Science and Human Health, January 11-14, 1993, Calcutta* (Calcutta: Tea Research Association, 1993), pp. 397-407.

220A Liang, Xuangiang. 'Status of Groundnut Cultivation and Production in Guangdong', in CLL Gowda, *et.al.* (Eds.),

Achieving High Groundnut Yields: Proceedings of an International Workshop, August 1995, Shandong Peanut Research Institute (SPRI), Laixi, Shandong, China (Patancheru: ICRISAT, 1996), pp. 217-22.

221 Mulky, Hemant. 'Japan Cotton Statistics', in *Indian Cotton Annual, 1993-94, No. 74* (Bombay: East India Cotton Association, 1994), pp. 192-94.

221A Qiu, Qingshu, *et.al.* 'Selection and Extension of High-yielding Groundnut Varieties in China', in CLL Gowda, *et.al.* (Eds.), *Achieving High Groundnut Yields: Proceedings of an International Workshop, August 1995, Shandong Peanut Research Institute (SPRI), Laixi, Shandong, China* (Patancheru: ICRISAT, 1996), pp. 141-46.

221B Sun, Yanhao, *et.al.*, 'Theoretical Foundations for High-Yielding Groundnut Varieties in China', in CLL Gowda, *et.al.* (Eds.), *Achieving High Groundnut Yields: Proceedings of an International Workshop, August 1995, Shandong Peanut Research Institute (SPRI), Laixi, Shandong, China* (Patancheru: ICRISAT, 1996), pp. 129-40.

-- Farming and Farming Research

222 Lui, Yanhua. 'Farmers' Strategies in the Mountain Areas of West Sichuan: China', in N.S. Jodha, *et.al.* (Eds.), *Sustainable Mountain Agriculture* (New Delhi: Oxford and IBH Publishing Company, 1992), Vol. 2, pp. 423-45.

223 Zuo, Mengxiao. 'China', in Regional Workshop on On-Farm Adapting Research (1993: Ho Chi Minh City), *Approaches to On-Farm Research in Asia* (Patancheru, A.P.: International Crops Research Institute for the Semi-Arid Tropics, 1993), pp. 89-91.

223A Cao, Zhihong. 'Balanced Fertilisation and Food Security in China', in FAI Seminar 1996: *Fertiliser and Agriculture, Emerging Compulsions: Papers Presented at the Seminar held at New Delhi During December 5-7, 1996* (New Delhi: Fertiliser Association of India, 1996), S-III-3(1-2).

223B Stauffer, M.D. and Beaton, James D. 'Importance of Plant Nutrients in Increasing Agricultural Productivity—Chinese Experience', in *FAI Seminar 1995: Structural Reforms and the Fertiliser Sector* (New Delhi: Fertiliser Association of India, 1996), S-III-3(1-19).

-- Food and Food Policy

224 Basu, Anuradha. 'Food Security Policies: A Comparative Study of India and China', in S.P. Gupta, *et.al.* (Eds.), *Development Patterns and Institutional Structures: China and India* (New Delhi: Allied Publishers, 1995).

225 Hu, Jiapeng. 'Clan in the People's Republic of China', in Clan Country Coordinators Consultative Meeting (1993: Patancheru, India). *Cereal and Legumes: An Asian Perspective* (Patancheru, Andhra Pradesh: ICRISAT, 1993), pp. 43-49.

226 Pudney, Stephen. 'Rationing and Consumer Demand in China: Simulating the Effects of Changes in the Food Subsidy System', in S.P. Gupta, *et.al.* (Eds.), *Development Patterns and Institutional Structures: China and India* (New Delhi: Allied Publishers, 1995), pp. 115-47.

-- Horticulture

227 Zhang, Du. 'Horticultural Development in the Himalaya and the Hengdun Mountains, China', in S.S. Teaotia (Ed.), *Horticultural Development in the Hindu Kush-Himalayan Region* (New Delhi: Oxford and IBH Publishing Company, 1993), pp. 247-88.

-- Irrigation

228 Hoshino, Emiko. 'Operation and Maintenance of Irrigation System and Strengthening of Farmers' Organization' in *16th International Congress on Irrigation and Drainage, Cairo, Egypt, 1996: Transactions* (New Delhi: International Commission on Irrigation and Drainage, 1996), pp. 95-111.

229 Huang, Baoquan, etc. 'Functions of Farmers' Water-Saving Association in Irrigation Management—An Investigation in Yuwang Township, Xiaxian, Shanxi', in *16th International Congress on Irrigation and Drainage, Cairo, Egypt, 1996: Transactions* (New Delhi: International Commission on Irrigation and Drainage, 1996), pp. 23-31.

230 Wang, Shaohua. 'The Basis of Irrigation and Drainage Zowing in the North of China', in *15th International Congress on Irrigation and Drainage The Hague, The*

Netherlands, 1993: Transactions (New Delhi: International Commission on Irrigation and Drainage, 1993), pp. 261-70.

231 Xu, Zhifang, *et.al.* 'Irrigation Management Transfer in China', in *16th International Congress on Irrigation and Drainage, Cairo, Egypt, 1996: Transactions* (New Delhi: International Commission on Irrigation and Drainage, 1996), pp. 57-66.

-- Land Tenure and Use

232 Ghose, Chitra. 'Land Degradation, Soil Erosion and Water Resource Management in China', in Chitra Ghose, *Development Redefined: The Crisis in Sustaining Agricultural Development* (Calcutta: Best Books, 1996), Vol. I, pp. 93-8.

233 Ghose, Chitra. 'Sustainable Agricultural Development and Land Use Planning in China', in Chitra Ghose, *Development Redefined: The Crisis in Sustaining Agricultural Development* (Calcutta: Best Books, 1996), Vol. I, pp. 87-92.

234 Jiang, Tong. 'Soil Erosion and Regional Ecological Management in the Headwater Area of Eastern China—A Case Study in the Tianwu Mountains', in Josef Krecek, *et.al.* (Eds.), *Hydrological Problems and Environmental Management in Highlands and Headwaters* (New Delhi: Oxford and IBH Publishing Company, 1996), pp. 35-42.

-- Marketing

235 Riethmuller, P. 'The Japanese Processed Food Market: An Australian Perspective', in Duo-Tho Nguyan and Kartic C. Roy (Eds.), *Economic Reform, Liberalisation and Trading in the Asia-Pacific Region* (New Delhi: Wiley Eastern, 1994), pp. 207-19.

-- Reforms

236 Elizondo, Hunberto Garza. 'Revolution and Agrarian Reform in China and Mexico', in Manoranjan Mohanty (Ed.), *Chinese Revolution: Comparative Perspectives on Transformation of Non-Western Societies* (Delhi: Ajanta Publications, 1992), pp. 235-60.

-- Regional Development Planning

237 Maithani, B.P. 'Management of Hill Area Development: Insights From Japanese Experience', in D.C. Pandey (Ed.), *Dimensions of Agriculture in the Himalaya* (Almora: Shri Almora Book Depot, 1996), pp. 161-81.

-- Rice Cultivation

238 Murty, V.V.N. 'Paddy Field Consolidation in Japan', in V.V.N. Murty and K. Takeuchi, *Land and Water Development For Agriculture in the Asia-Pacific Region* (New Delhi: Oxford and IBH Publishing Company, 1996), pp. 77-81.

-- Technological Change

239 Husain, Majid. 'The China-Japan Genecentre', in Majid Husain, *Systematic Agricultural Geography* (Jaipur: Rawat Publications, 1996), p. 55.

240 Li, Zhengzheng. 'China: Qianxian Biovillage', in M.S. Swaminathan, *Biotechnology in Agriculture: A Dialogue : Reaching the Unreached* (Madras: Macmillan India, 1991), pp. 351-60.

- COMPARATIVE DEVELOPMENT

241 Kelkar, Vijay L. and Rao, V.V.B. (Eds.), 'India and East Asia in a Comparative Perspective', in Vijay L. Kelkar and V.V.B. Rao (Eds.), *India: Development Policy Imperatives* (New Delhi: Tata McGraw-Hill Publishing Company, 1996), pp. 70-79.

- COOPERATIVES AND COOPERATIVISATION

242 Hu, Jiapeng and Yang, Yan. 'China', in C.L.L. Gowda and A. Ramakrishna (Eds.), *CLAN Cooperative Research in Asia: Needs and Opportunities* (Patancheru: ICRISAT, 1996), pp. 24-7.

243 Ohya, Masao. 'The Japanese Experience', in *Report of the ICA/NCCT/NCCF Raiqad Bazar Regional Workshop on Modern Management of Consumers, Cooperatives For South and South East Asia, 1995, Alibag, India* (New Delhi: International Cooperative Alliance, Regional Office for South Asia and the Pacific, 1996), pp. 73-78 .

- COMMUNICATIONS AND TRANSPORT

244 Garg, Y.M. 'Coping with Transport Needs: The Japanese Way', in Suman Chopra, *et.al.* (Eds.), *Railway Yearbook, 1992* (New Delhi: Suman Chopra, 1992), pp. 35-38.

245 Garg, Y.M. 'Japanese Railway System', in Suman Chopra, *et.al.* (Eds.), *Railway Yearbook, 1992* (New Delhi: Suman Chopra, 1992), pp. 23-31.

246 Lam, Albert K.Y. 'Hong Kong Ventures', in S.S. Sidhu (Ed.), *New Horizons in Travel and Tourism: Asian Approach* (New Delhi: Har-Anand Publications, 1996), pp. 68-74.

- ECONOMIC DEMOGRAPHY

247 Hussain, Athar. 'On the Recent Increase in Death Rates in China', in S.P. Gupta, *et.al.* (Eds.), *Development Patterns and Institutional Structures: China and India* (New Delhi: Allied Publishers, 1995), pp. 207-22.

- ECONOMIC HISTORY

248 Raghava Varior, M.R. 'Trade Relations Between Kerala and China 1200-1500 A.D.', in *Proceedings of the Indian History Congress, 51st Session, Calcutta University, Calcutta, 1990* (Delhi: Indian History Congress, 1991), pp. 690-98.

249 Rougeulle, Axelle. 'Medieval Trade Networks in the Western Indian Ocean (8-14 Centuries): Some Reflections from the Distribution of Chinese Imports in the Islamic World', in Himanshu Praba Ray and Jean-Francois Salles (Eds.), *Tradition and Archaeology: Early Maritime Contacts in the Indian Ocean: Proceedings of International Seminar, Techno-Archaeological Perspectives of Seafaring in the Indian Ocean, 4th Cent. B.C.—15th Cent. A.D.* (New Delhi: Manohar Publishers and Distributors, 1996), pp. 159-80.

- ECONOMIC PLANNING

250 Banerjee, Pranab K. 'On Planned Development in India and China', in B. Satyanarayan (Ed.), *A Comparative Study of Foreign Direct Investment in China and India* (Bombay: Himalaya Publishing House, 1996), pp. 139-51.

251 Narasimulu, M. and Sudhakar Reddy, B. 'The Overall Planned Development Strategies in India and China

with Special Reference to Foreign Direct Investment', in B. Satyanarayan (Ed.), *A Comparative Study of Foreign Direct Investment in China and India* (Bombay: Himalaya Publishing House, 1996), pp. 107-13.

- ECONOMIC POLICY

252 Gao, Hongbin. 'Anti-Poverty Focussed Programmes in the Mountains: Experiences in China', in N.S. Jodha, *et.al.* (Eds.), *Sustainable Mountain Agriculture* (Delhi: Oxford and IBH Publishing Company, 1992), Vol. 2, pp. 591-96.

- ECONOMIC REFORMS

253 Ahluwalia, Isher Judge. 'Economic Liberalisation: Chinese Development Experience', in Ashok Bapua (Ed.), *One World or No World: Sustainable Development Strategies for the 21st Century* (Jaipur: Society for International Development, Rajasthan Chapter, 1994), pp. 144-50.

254 Ajit Singh. 'The Plan, The Market and Evolutionary Economic Reform in China', in Abu Abdullah, *et.al.* (Eds.), *State, Market and Development: Essays in Honour of Rehman Sobhan* (New Delhi: Oxford University Press, 1996), pp. 193-203.

255 Bharadwaj, Ram Dev. 'China's Strategy for Economic Reforms and Modernization', in A.D.N. Bajpai (Ed.), *Emerging Trends in Indian Economy: Papers in Honour of Professor Daya Shankar Nag* (New Delhi: Atlantic, 1995), pp. 109-16.

256 Cherunilam, Francis. 'Economic Reforms in China', in Francis Cherunilam, *Economic Reforms in India and Abroad* (Bombay: Himalaya Publishing House, 1992), pp. 5-10.

257 Debroy, Dipavali. 'An Overview of China's Economic Reforms', in Bibek Debroy (Ed.), *China's External Trade Since the Reforms* (New Delhi: Commonwealth Publishers, 1991), pp. 31-54.

258 Debroy, Dipavalis. 'Some Implications of the Economic Reforms With Special Reference to Welfare Aspects', in Bibek Debroy (Ed.), *China's External Trade Since the*

Reforms (New Delhi: Commonwealth Publishers, 1991), pp. 55-73.

259 Guo, Shuqing. 'From a Closed Economy to an Open Economy: An Important Profile of China's Economic Reform', in S.P. Gupta, *et.al.* (Eds.), *Trade Policy Reform* (New Delhi: Indian Council for Research on International Economic Relations; Macmillan, 1994), pp. 89-93.

260 Gupta, S.P. 'China's Economic Reforms: Features, Performance and Prospects', in S.P. Gupta, *The Role of Special Economic Zones and Economic and Technological Development Zones* (New Delhi: Allied Publishers, 1996), pp. 1-31.

261 Gupta, S.P. 'Economic Reform in China and India: A Comparison', in S.P. Gupta, *et.al.* (Eds.), *Development Patterns and Institutional Structures: China and India* (New Delhi: Allied Publishers, 1995), pp. 355-62.

262 Gupta, S.P. and Singh, Alaka. 'Economic Reform in China and India: A Comparison', in Tan Chung (Ed.), *India and China* (New Delhi: Indian Council for Cultural Relations, 1994), pp. 269-77; *Indian Horizons*: Special Issue, Vol. 43, Nos. 1-2, 1994.

263 Manimekalai, N. 'Indo-China Socio-Economic Background—Compared', in B. Satyanarayan (Ed.), *A Comparative Study of Foreign Direct Investment in China and India* (Bombay: Himalaya Publishing House, 1996), pp. 169-81.

264 Mao, Yu-shi. 'An Institutional Perspective on Socialist Economic Reforms, the Chinese Experience', in Kartikey C. Roy, *et.al. Economic Development of Poor Countries: Experiences, Obstacles and Sustainability in Global Perspectives* (Calcutta: International Institute for Development Studies, 1991), pp. 123-41.

265 Mishra, Girish. 'Japan: Before and After the Meiji Restoration' and 'State and Economic Development in Japan', in Girish Mishra, *Comparative Economic Development* (Delhi: Pragati Publications, 1996), pp. 154-89.

266 Pick, Hannah. 'Chinese Transformation: Continuity and Change', in P. Tehral and J.G. De Vries (Eds.), *Development, Transformation and State Policy* (New Delhi: Manohar Publishers and Distributors, 1995), pp. 301-30.

267 Roy, K.C. 'Economic Liberalisation and the Delivery of Public Goods to the Poor: A Study of India and China', in Duo-Tho Nguyen and Kartic C. Roy (Eds.), *Economic Reform, Liberalisation and Trade in the Asia-Pacific Region* (New Delhi: Wiley Eastern, 1994), pp. 31-48.

268 Saith, Ashwani. Rural Bases of Successful Transition: Some Chinese Lessons for Reforming and Developing Economics', in P. Tehral and J.G. De Vries (Eds.), *Development, Transformation and State Policy* (New Delhi: Manohar Publishers and Distributors, 1995), pp. 79-107 .

269 Shah, Maya. 'Economic Reforms and Foreign Direct Investment in India and China', in B. Satyanarayan (Ed.), *A Comparative Study of Foreign Direct Investment in China and India* (Bombay: Himalaya Publishing House, 1996), pp. 91-106.

270 Shi, Min. 'The Model of Economic Reform in a Developing Socialist Country: Practice of Economic Reform and Opening in China', in V.R. Panchamukhi and Rehman Sobhan (Eds.), *Towards An Asian Economic Area* (New Delhi: Macmillan, 1995), pp. 120-37.

271 Shiva Ramu, S. 'The Giant Dragon: China: Economic Reforms', in S. Shiva Ramu, *The Dragons of Asia: Asia-Pacific Rim Countries and Their Multinationals* (New Delhi: A.H. Wheeler and Company, 1995), pp. 59-112.

272 Tripathi, S.D. 'China's Economic Development and the Maoist Strategy: Indian Perspectives', in S.D. Tripathi, *Perspectives in Indian Management* (Jaipur: Arihant Publishers, 1992), Vol. 1, pp. 30-41.

273 Zheng, Zemin. 'The Chinese Economy and the Revolutionary Process', in Manoranjan Mohanty (Ed.), *Chinese Revolution: Comparative Perspectives on Transformation of Non-Western Societies* (Delhi: Ajanta Publications, 1992), pp. 65-94.

- ECONOMIC SITUATION

274 Ajit Singh. *How East Asia Grew So Fast?: Slow Progress Towards An Analytical Consensus* (New Delhi: Research and Information System for Non-Aligned and Other Developing Countries, 1995).

275 Banerjee, Kashitish Chandra. 'Comparative Performance of Japan and Others', in Kashitish Chandra Banerjee, *The Glimpses of Great Thoughts* (Calcutta: K.C. Banerjee, 1995), pp. 173-78.

276 Bharadwaj, Ram Dev. *China's Economic Liberalization* (New Delhi: Lancers Books, 1995).

277 Chacko, K.C. *Economic Development of India and Japan* (New Delhi: Vikas, 1993).

278 Chai, C.H. 'Recent Developments in China and its Implications for the Asia-Pacific Region', in Fu-chen Lo and Narongchai Akrasanee (Eds.), *The Future of Asia-Pacific Economics: Emerging Role of Asian NIES and ASEAN: Papers and Proceedings of the Conference held in November 1989 in Bangkok* (New Delhi: Allied Publishers, 1992), pp. 246-68.

279 'China', in *Aiding Globalisation Process of Indian Business: Select Country Profiles* (New Delhi: Associated Chambers of Commerce and Industry of India, 1994), pp. 24-33.

280 *China's Open Economy: Development and Growth* (New Delhi: Research Department, Confederation of Indian Industry, 1995).

281 Clark, Cal. 'State and Market in the Development of Taiwan's Island Economy', in Gabby Rony, *et.al.* (Eds.), *Economics of Small Island Nations* (New Delhi: New Age International, 1996), pp. 249-67.

282 Dutta, Rakhal. 'Chinese Economic Development and its Lessons', in Asim Chaudhuri, *Economic Development as a Subject for Teaching and Research: Papers Presented at the Summer Institute on Economic Development as a subject for Teaching and Research Held at Calcutta During 27 March to 9 May 1985* (Calcutta: Department of Economics, Rabindra Bharati University, 1994), pp. 175-79.

283 Deb, Kalipada. *The Chinese Economy: Changes and Challenges in the Post-Mao Era* (New Delhi: M.D. Publications, 1993).

284 *Development for Whom?: A Report on the Chinese Development Strategies in Tibet and Their Impacts* (Dharamsala: Tibetan Youth Congress, Office of the Central Executive Committee, 1995).

285 Dreze, Jean and Sen, Amartya. 'India and China', in *India: Economic Development and Social Opportunity* (Delhi: Oxford University Press, 1995), pp. 57-86.

286 Feng, Yushu. 'China's Economic Performance and Prospects for the Future', in V.R. Panchamukhi and Rehman Sobhan (Eds.), *Towards an Asian Economic Area* (New Delhi: Macmillan, 1995), pp. 138-40.

286A Gurdip Singh, *Doing Business With Korea* (New Delhi: Himalaya Publishers, 1995).

287 Harsh Mander Singh. 'Observations on Present-Day Political Economy', in Carr-Harris Jill and Niloy Banerjee (Eds.), *China Country Report* (New Delhi: South-South Solidarity, 1996), pp. 1-10.

288 Hussain, Athar. 'Growth Patterns and Structural Changes in the Chinese Economy', in S.P. Gupta, *et.al.* (Eds.), *Development Patterns and Institutional Structures: China and India* (New Delhi: Allied Publishers, 1995), pp. 18-44.

288A Kelkar, Vijay L. and Bhanoji Rao, V.V. 'India and East Asia in a Comparative Perspective', in Vijay L. Kelkar and V.V. Bhanoji Rao (Eds.), *India: Development Policy Imperatives* (New Delhi: Tata McGraw-Hill Publishing Company, 1996), pp. 70-79.

289 Nagami, K. 'Maturing of the Japanese Economy in the 1980s', in P.R. Shukla and S.K. Roy Chowdhry (Eds.), *Select Issues in Economic Development* (New Delhi: Akashdeep Publishing House, 1992), pp. 245-61.

290 Norbu, Dawa. 'Changes in Tibetan Economy, 1959-76', in Ranju K. Dhamala, *Problems and Strategies of Development in the Eastern Himalaya* (New Delhi: Gyan Publishing House, 1993), pp. 53-74.

291 Palaha, Satinder. 'The Service Economy in China', in Bibek Debroy (Ed.), *China's External Trade Since the Reforms* (New Delhi: Commonwealth Publishers, 1991), pp. 349-82.

292 Park, Yung Chul and Chung, Ki-Young. 'Economic Cooperation and Integration in East Asia', in V.R. Panchamukhi and Rehman Sobhan (Eds.), *Towards An Asian Economic Area* (New Delhi: Macmillan, 1995), pp. 361-71.

293 Pudney, Stephen. 'The Pattern of Consumer Demand in China', in S.P. Gupta, *et.al.* (Eds.), *Development Patterns and Institutional Structures: China and India* (New Delhi: Allied Publishers, 1995), pp. 148-70.

294 *Seminar on Doing Business With China: Opportunities for Indian Entrepreneurs: Background Paper* (New Delhi: Confederation of Indian Industry, 1995).

295 Wienbaum, Batya. 'How Capital Invades Women's Share of Production in China', in Maithreyi Krishna Raj, *Gender in Economics: Theory and Practice* (New Delhi: Ajanta Publications, 1993), pp. 48-53.

- ECONOMIC STATISTICS

296 Mulky, Hemant (Comp.). 'Japan Cotton Statistics', in Hemant Mulky (Comp.), *Indian Cotton Annual 1994-95, No. 75* (Bombay: East India Cotton Association, 1995), pp. 175-77.

- ECONOMIC THOUGHTS

297 Ghosh, B.N. 'Maoist Model of Development', in B.N. Ghosh. *Political Economy of Development and Underdevelopment: Appraisal of Radical Theories* (New Delhi: Deep and Deep Publications, 1996), pp. 14-26.

- FINANCIAL SERVICES

298 Shiva Ramu, S. 'Japanese Institutions', in S. Shiva Ramu, *Global Financial Services Industry* (Delhi: South Asia Publications, 1995), pp. 352-59.

299 Srikrishna, V. 'Japanese Financial System', in P.R. Shukla, S.K. Roy Chowdhury (Eds.), *Select Issues in*

Economic Development (New Delhi: Akashdeep Publishing House, 1992), pp. 261-78.

300 Trivedi, H.K. 'Financial Reforms in Japan and India: A Comparative View', in Sushil J. Lalwani (Ed.), *Security Market in India* (Jodhpur: Books Treasure, 1994), pp. 58-66.

301 Wu, Jing Lian. 'China: Intergovernmental Fiscal Relations and Macro—Economic Management', in S.P. Gupta, *et.al.* (Eds.), *Intergovernmental Fiscal Relations and Macroeconomic Management in Large Countries* (New Delhi: Allied, 1994), pp. 231-68.

- BANKS AND BANKING

302 Bhatt, V.V. 'The Main Bank System in Japan: Financial Innovation for Industrial Development', in V.V. Bhatt, *Financial Systems, Innovations and Development* (New Delhi: Sage Publications, 1995), pp. 66-105.

303 'Export-Import Bank of China', in *Exim Banks in Asia: A Comparative Analysis* (New Delhi: New Age International, 1996), pp. 102-05.

304 'Export-Import Bank of Japan', in *Exim Banks in Asia: A Comparative Analysis* (New Delhi: New Age International, 1996), pp. 31-49.

305 'Export-Import Bank of Taiwan', in *Exim Banks in Asia: A Comparative Analysis* (New Delhi: New Age International, 1996), pp. 67-77.

306 He, Lixiang. 'Services Offered by Agricultural Bank of China', in Chakradhari Agrawal (Ed.), *SMEs Towards 2000: A Collection of Papers Presented at the 6th International Conference of Small Medium Enterprises held at Seoul in April 1992—The World Conference of Small and Medium Enterprises Held at Beijing in March 1993* (New Delhi: Publications Divisions, World Assembly of Small and Medium Enterprises, 1993), pp. 84-87.

-- Investment

307 Ho, Yan-ki. 'Hong Kong, Singapore and Taiwan as New Financial Centres', in Fu-chen Lo and Narongchai Akrasanee, *The Future of Asia-Pacific Economics: Emerging Role of Asian NIES and ASEAN: Papers and Proceedings of*

the Conference Held in November 1989 in Bangkok (New Delhi: Allied, 1992), pp. 432-80.

- HOUSING

308 Gupta, R.G. 'Housing in China', in R.G. Gupta, *Shelter For Poor in the Fourth World* (Delhi: Shipra Publications, 1995), pp. 24-31.

309 Lai, On-Kwok. 'The Logic of Urban Development and Slum Settlements: The People's Republic of China', in On-Kwok Lai, *Housing the Urban Poor: Policy and Practice in Developing Countries* (New Delhi: Vistaar Publications, 1995), pp. 277-92.

310 Smart, Alan. 'Hong Kong's Slums and Squatter Areas: A Developmental Perspective', in On-Kwok Lai, *Housing the Urban Poor: Policy and Practice in Developing Countries* (New Delhi: Vistaar Publications, 1995), pp. 97-111.

- INDUSTRIES AND INDUSTRIALISATION

311 Abraham, Biju Paul. 'West Germany and Japan: The Debate on Industrial Competitiveness', in K.B. Lall, *et.al.* (Eds.), *European Union and Transformation of Europe's Economy* (New Delhi: Radiant Publishers, 1993), pp. 220-31.

312 Dhaul, Harry. 'Models Linking Ecological Security With Livelihood Security—Rural Enterprises in China and India', in M.S. Swaminathan (Ed.), *Ecotechnology and Rural Employment: A Dialogue* (Madras: Macmillan, 1994), pp. 113-19.

313 He, Kang. 'The Spark Programme and Rural Township Enterprises in China', in M.S. Swaminathan (Ed.), *Ecotechnology and Rural Employment: A Dialogue* (Madras: Macmillan, 1994), pp. 142-65.

314 Jani, B.N. 'Process of Industrialisation in Chinese Economy', in B. Satyanarayan (Ed.), *A Comparative Study of Foreign Direct Investment in China and India* (Bombay: Himalaya Publishing House, 1996), pp. 247-54.

315 Kotaiah, P. 'Report on SPARK Programme for Rural Industrialisation, China', in P. Kotaiah, *A Policy Package For Rural Industrialisation* (Bombay: National Bank for Agriculture and Rural Development, 1995), pp. 34-47.

316 Reddy, G. Pakki. 'Rural Industrialisation and Poverty Alleviation: Lessons From the Chinese Experience', in Shobha Raghuram, *et.al.* (Eds.), *Structural Adjustment: Economy, Environment, Social Concerns* (New Delhi: Macmillan, 1995), pp. 117-31.

317 Song, Zehon. A New Approach to Rural Industrialization—Relevant Policies of China's Spark Program', in Chakradhari Agrawal (Ed.), *SMEs Towards 2000: A Collection of Papers Presented at the 6th International Conference of Small Medium Enterprises held at Seoul in April 1992—The World Conference of Small and Medium Enterprises Held at Beijing in March 1993* (New Delhi: Publications Divisions, World Assembly of Small and Medium Enterprises, 1993), pp. 230-35.

318 Zhang, Xueyang. 'Study of the Optimization of the Industrial Development and Environmental Protection in Shijizhuang City', in R.S. Nirjar (Ed.), *Proceedings: Icomen-91: International Conference on Man and Environment, 14-16 December 1991: Conference In Print* (Allahabad: Department of Civil Engineering, Moti Lal Nehru Regional Engineering College, 1994), pp. 143-54.

319 Zheng, Zhaoiao. 'The Position, Role and Developing Trend of Chinese Small and Medium Enterprises (SMEs), in Chakradhari Agrawal (Ed.), *SMEs Towards 2000: A Collection of Papers Presented at the 6th International Conference of Small Medium Enterprises held at Seoul in April 1992—The World Conference of Small and Medium Enterprises Held at Beijing in March 1993* (New Delhi: Publications Divisions, World Assembly of Small and Medium Enterprises, 1993), pp. 245-48.

- DIVISIONS OF INDUSTRIES

-- Automobiles

320 Kathuria, Sanjay. 'The Japanese Example', in Sanjay Kathuria, *Competing Through Technology and Manufacturing: A Study of Indian Commercial Vehicles Industry* (Delhi: Oxford University Press, 1996), pp. 43-47.

-- Computers

321 'China, Japan, Taiwan', in *A Comparative Study on Computer Industry in Far—Eastern Countries* (New Delhi: MAIT, 1994), pp. 13-28, 44-59.

-- Electronics and Electricals

322 'Chinese Television Industry: The Interaction Between Government Policy and Market Forces', in S.P. Gupta, *et.al.* (Eds.), *Development Patterns and Institutional Structures: China and India* (New Delhi: Allied Publishers, 1995), pp. 315-54.

323 Jain, Ashok. *Industrialization in India and China: A Comparative Study of Machine Building and Electronic Industries* (New Delhi: Har-Anand Publications, 1995)..

- Fishing Industry

324 Dai, Tianyuan, *et.al.* 'An Approach to Trawl Fishery Management in the Taiwan Strait From the Engineering Economic Point of Views', in Robert M. Meyer, *et.al.* (Eds.), *Fisheries Resource Utilization and Policy: Proceedings of the World Fisheries Congress, Theme 2* (New Delhi: Oxford and IBH Publishing Company, 1996), pp. 418-30.

325 Jianking, Ye, *et.al.* 'An Economic-Engineering Approach to Analyze Light Seiners in the Taiwan Strait', in Robert M. Meyer, *et.al.* (Eds.), *Fisheries Resource Utilization and Policy: Proceedings of the World Fisheries Congress, Theme 2* (New Delhi: Oxford and IBH Publishing Company, 1996), pp. 431-39.

326 Wing, Han-ping. 'A Review of the Bionomics, Population Dynamics, and Management of the Reeves Shad in the Yangtze River', in Robert M. Meyer, *et.al.* (Eds.), *Fisheries Resource Utilization and Policy: Proceedings of the World Fisheries Congress, Theme 2* (New Delhi: Oxford and IBH Publishing Company, 1996), pp. 147-55.

-- Gem and Jewellery

327 Kala, Vidya Vinod. 'China' and 'Japan' in Vidya Vinod Kala (Ed.), *Gem and Jewellery Year Book, 1995* (Jaipur: International Journal House, 1995), pp. 251-52, 294-300.

328 Kala, Vidya Vinod. 'Glimpses of World Gems Centres: China' in Vidya Vinod Kala, *et.al.* (Eds.), *Gem and Jewellery Year Book, 1993-94* (Jaipur: International Journal House, 1994), pp. 236-37.

329 Kala, Vidya Vinod. 'Glimpses of World Gems Centres: Japan' in Vidya Vinod Kala, *et.al.* (Eds.), *Gem and Jewellery Year Book, 1993-94* (Jaipur: International Journal House, 1994), pp. 278-86.

-- Hydropower Plants

330 Cheng, Xialei. 'Automation of SHP in China' in Central Board of Irrigation and Power. *Course, Small Hydro-Development, 21-26 August 1995, New Delhi: Proceedings* (New Delhi: Central Board of Irrigation and Power, 1995), pp. 347-51.

331 Mei, Zu-yan. 'Hydro Power Development in China', in *International Conference on Power Development in Afro-Asian Countries, New Delhi, 10-14 December 1990: Technical Papers* (New Delhi: International Association on Electricity Generation, Transmission, and Distribution, Afro-Asian Region, 1990), Vol. 1, pp. 101-11.

332 Tong, Jiangdong and Cheng, Xialei, 'Sustainable SHP Development in China', in Central Board of Irrigation and Power. *Course, Small Hydro-Development, 21-26 August 1995, New Delhi: Proceedings* (New Delhi: Central Board of Irrigation and Power, 1995), pp. 323-28.

333 Zhang, Boting. 'Small Hydropower Development in China', in C.V.J. Varma (Ed.), *International R and D Conference, Water and Energy 2001: Needs, Development, Utilization, Diamond Jubilee Research and Development Session, New Delhi, India, October 1995* (New Delhi: Oxford and IBH Publishing Company, 1996), pp. 226-34.

-- Iron and Steel

334 D'Mello, Bernard. *Technological Backwardness or Technological Dependence: The Relative Performance of the China and South Korean Steel Industries* (Calcutta: Indian Institute of Management, 1992).

335 Etienne, Gilbert. *Asian Crucible: The Steel Industry in China and India* (New Delhi: Sage Publications, 1992).

-- Mining and Metals

336 Zhihong, L. 'High-Output and High-Efficiency in Coal Mines of China', in U. Kumar (Ed.), *High Production Technology For Underground Mines* (Calcutta: Mining, Geological and Metallurgical Institute of India, 1996), pp. 315-32.

-- Plastics Industry

337 Vyas, Jay Narayan and Pandya, D.L. (Eds.) 'Japan', in Jay Narayan Vyas and D.L. Pandya (Eds.), *Saket International Directory of Plastics Technology and Machinery* (Ahmedabad: Saket Communication Centre, 1996), pp. 77-79.

-- Silk Industry

338 Murakami, T. 'Challenges to Sericulture Industry of Japan in 21st Century', in A.K. Ganguly (Ed.), *International Conference on Sericulture: Global Silk Scenario 2001, October 1994: Souvenir* (Mysore: Central Sericultural Research and Training Institute; International Centre for Training and Research in Tropical Sericulture, 1994), pp. 9-12.

-- Telecom Industry

339 Rao, J. Rajeshwar. 'Foreign Direct Investment and Development of Telecom Sectors: A Comparative Study of India and China', in B. Satyanarayan (Ed.), *A Comparative Study of Foreign Direct Investment in China and India* (Bombay: Himalaya Publishing House, 1996), pp. 182-97.

- ENERGY RESOURCES

340 Desai, Ashok V. *Energy in China* (New Delhi: Wiley Eastern, 1990).

341 Furugaki, Issei. 'Energy Conservation in Japan—Present Status and Prospects', in C.P. Moraes (Ed.), *Energy Conservation Directory* (Bombay: Astra Publishers, 1992), pp. 37-47.

342 Matsuo, M. 'Japan', in R.K. Pichauri and Preeti Bhandari (Eds.), *Global Warming: Collaborative Study on Strategies to Limit CC2 Emissions in Asia and Brazil* (New

Delhi: Asian Energy Institute; Tata McGraw-Hill Publishing Company, 1992), pp. 103-49.

343 Matsuura, Kazuo. 'Japan: Energy and the Environment', in Preeti Soni (Ed.), *Energy and Environmental Challenges in Central Asia and the Caucassus: Windows For Cooperation* (New Delhi: Tata Energy Research Institute, 1996), pp. 189-97.

344 Qian, Zhengying (Ed.). *Water Resources Development in China* (Beijing: China Water and Power Press; and New Delhi: Central Board of Irrigation and Power, 1994).

345 *Waste Resource Recycling by Cooperatives: The Chinese Experience: Report of ICA Regional Workshop, Shanghai (China), 25 March—4 April 1991* (New Delhi: International Cooperative Alliance, Regional Office for Asia and the Pacific, 1991).

346 Zongxin, W. 'China', in R.K. Pichauri and Preeti Bhandari (Eds.), *Global Warming: Collaborative Study on Strategies to Limit CC2 Emissions in Asia and Brazil* (New Delhi: Asian Energy Institute; Tata McGraw-Hill Publishing Coppany, 1992), pp. 45-63.

- INDUSTRIAL GROWTH

347 Kothari, S.S. 'Role of Technology for Growth: Japan's Strategy—A Success Story', in S.S. Kothari, *New Fiscal and Economic Strategies for Growth in Developing Countries* (Delhi: Oxford University Press, 1992), pp. 173-78.

348 Om Prakash. 'Industrial Growth in China', in Om Prakash, *Development and Fiscal Economics* (Jaipur: RBSA Publishers, 1992), pp. 42-69.

349 Shi, Zulin and Liu, Deshun. 'China: Socio-economy, Energy and the Environment', in Preeti Soni (Ed.), *Energy and Environmental Challenges in Central Asia and the Caucassus: Windows For Cooperation* (New Delhi: Tata Energy Research Institute, 1996), pp. 143-60.

-INDUSTRIAL MANAGEMENT

350 Antoniou, Peter H. and Whitman, Katherine. 'The Preference of Chinese Managers for Work Related Rewards', in Jagjit Singh (Ed.), *Marketing and Management Co-operation with the Asia-Pacific Region*

(New Delhi: Institute of Marketing and Management, 1990), pp. 129-40.

351 Bhattacharya, B. *Winning the World Market: Strategies for Success: How to Use the Japanese Technique to Succeed in the Global Market* (Delhi: Global Business Press, 1994).

352 Chao, Y.T. 'Culture and Work Organization: The Chinese Case', in Henry S.R. Rao, *et.al.* (Eds.), *Effective Organizations and Social Values* (New Delhi: Sage Publications, 1994), pp. 28-36.

353 Chatterjee, Bhaskar. *Japanese Management: Maruti and the Indian Experience* (New Delhi: Sterling Publishers, 1990).

354 Chatterjee, Bhaskar. *Japanese Management and the Indian Experience* (New Delhi: Sterling Publishers, 1992).

355 Gupta, C.B. 'Japanese Management and Theory', in C.B. Gupta, *Contemporary Management* (New Delhi: Ashish Publishing House, 1992).

356 Hwang, Kwang-Kuo. 'Modernization of the Chinese Family Business', in Henry S.R. Rao, *et.al.* (Eds.), *Effective Organizations and Social Values* (New Delhi: Sage Publications, 1994), pp. 37-62.

357 Jaspal Singh. 'Japanese Management', in Jaspal Singh, *Society, Culture and Socio-cultural Change* (New Delhi: National Book Organization, 1996), pp. 285-87.

358 Joshi, P.R. 'Japanese Capital Markets', in P.R. Joshi, *Global Capital Markets: Shopping For Finance* (New Delhi: Tata McGraw-Hill Publishing Company, 1996), pp. 47-69.

359 Jou, Jacob Yin-heng. 'Chinese Value System and Managerial Behaviour', in Henry S.R. Rao, *et.al.* (Eds.), *Effective Organizations and Social Values* (New Delhi: Sage Publications, 1994), pp. 63-71.

360 Ling, Wanquan. 'Theories on Leadership and Chinese Culture: The Formulation of the CPM Model on Leadership Behaviour and a Chinese Implicit Theory on Leadership Traits', in Henry S.R. Rao, *et.al.* (Eds.), *Effective Organizations and Social Values* (New Delhi: Sage Publications, 1994), pp. 269-86.

361 Meera Lal. 'The Japanse Experience', in Meera Lal, *Quality Management Through Quality Circles: An Indian Model* (Delhi: B.R. Publishing Corporation, 1994), pp. 29-35.

362 Mishra, M. 'Essentials of Japanese Management', in P.R. Shukla and S.K. Roy Choudhry (Eds.), *Select Issues in Economic Development* (New Delhi: Akashdeep Publishing House, 1992), pp. 299-321.

363 Misumi, Jyuji. 'The Japanese Meaning of Work and Small-Group Activities in Japanese Industrial Organizations', in Henry S.R. Rao, *et.al.* (Eds.), *Effective Organizations and Social Values* (New Delhi: Sage Publications, 1994), pp. 256-68.

364 Mittal, S.K. 'Japanese Management—Guidelines for Indian Industries', in B.L. Mathur (Ed.), *General Management* (Jaipur: Arihant Publishing House, 1994), pp. 167-76.

365 Murthy, D.B.N. 'The Japanese Obsession: Let's Do it Our Way', in D.B.N. Murthy, *Of Man and Management* (New Delhi: UBS Publishers' Distributors, 1995), pp. 187-90.

366 Peng, Jingfang. 'The China Information System for Enterprise Production and Circulation', in N. Seshagiri, *et.al.* (Eds.), *Information Systems for Economies in Transition: Papers Presented at the International Conference, ISET-IC, March 4-7, 1996, Ghaziabad, India* (New Delhi: Tata McGraw-Hill Publishing Company, 1996), pp. 128-35.

367 Rahman, Mustafa A. 'Total Productivity Management for Productivity Improvement: Lessons of Experience From a Japanese Manufacturing Company', in Dharni P. Sinha and Bhagwan Prasad (Eds.), *Redeployment of Labour in South Asia* (Hyderabad: Association of Management Development Institutions in South Asia, 1995), pp. 58-67.

368 Rao, Henry S.R. 'Cultural Adaptations and Diffusion for Managerial Strategies and Responses in Hong Kong', in Henry S.R. Rao, *et.al.* (Eds.), *Effective Organizations and Social Values* (New Delhi: Sage Publications, 1994), pp. 100-16.

369 Rastogi, P.N. 'Coping with Continuous Change—The Structure of the Japanese Innovation System', in P.N. Rastogi, *Management of Technology and Innovation; Competing Through Technological Excellence* (New Delhi: Sage Publications, 1995), pp. 255-75.

370 Redding, S.G. 'An Empirical Study of Overseas Chinese Managerial Ideology', in Henry S.R. Rao, *et.al.* (Eds.), *Effective Organizations and Social Values* (New Delhi: Sage Publications, 1994), pp. 72-84.

371 Sapre, S.A. 'Productivity in Japan: Lessons for India', in P.R. Shukla, *et.al.* (Eds.), *Development, Determinants and Alternatives* (New Delhi: Akashdeep Publishing House, 1992), pp. 261-76.

372 Swamy, S.A. *Trade and Industry in Japan: A Guide to Indian Entrepreneurs and Businessmen* (New Delhi: Prentice-Hall of India, 1993).

373 Thirunarayanan, R. 'Japanese Enterprises: What Make Them So Successful?', in J.K. Tandon, *et.al.* (Eds.), *Indian Management* (Jaipur: Arihant Publishing House, 1966), Vol. I, pp. 65-70.

374 Tripathi, Kamla Kant. *Road to Excellence: Japanese Management in Indian Milieu* (Delhi: Konark Publishers, 1994).

375 Zhang, Shou and Wang, Guizhen. 'Developing China's Information Industry to Accelerate Socialist Market Economic Growth', in N. Seshagiri, *et.al.* (Eds.), *Information Systems for Economies in Transition: Papers Presented at the International Conference, ISET-IC, March 4-7, 1996, Ghaziabad, India* (New Delhi: Tata McGraw-Hill Publishing Company, 1996), pp. 259-62.

376 Zhao, Ya Wen. 'Motivation Theory and Application in China: An Overview', in Henry S.R. Rao, *et.al.* (Eds.), *Effective Organizations and Social Values* (New Delhi: Sage Publications, 1994), pp. 115-31.

- INDUSTRIAL POLICY

377 Miyazaki, Isamu. 'Relationship Between the Government and Private Sector—Japanese Experience', in P.R. Shukla and S.K. Roy Chowdhury (Eds.), *Select*

Issues in Economic Development (New Delhi: Akashdeep Publishing House, 1992), pp. 278-98.

- TECHNOLOGICAL POLICY AND TRANSFER

378 Bischoff, Jurgen. *Chinese Technology Showcase, 8-11 April 1996, New Delhi: Technology Compendium* (New Delhi: Asian and Pacific Centre for Transfer of Technology of the Economic and Social Commission for Asia and the Pacific, 1996).

379 Bischoff, Jurgen. 'List of Products and Technologies From China', in *Chinese Technology Showcase, 8-11 April 1996, New Delhi: Technology Compendium* (New Delhi: Asian and Pacific Centre for Transfer of Technology of the Economic and Social Commission for Asia and the Pacific, 1996), pp. 167-68.

380 Khan, Mohsin U. *India and Korea: A Comparison of Electronic Technology Policy* (New Delhi: Har-Anand Publications, 1997).

381 'Science, Technology and Development: Lessons from India and China', in Pran Luthra (Ed.), *Dynamics of Technology Transfer and Industrialisation* (New Delhi: Commonwealth Publishers, 1995), pp. 132-61.

382 Simon, Denis Fred. 'The Emerging Technological Trajectory of the Pacific Rim Nations: Creating Competitive Advantage in the NICs and China', in Fu-chen Lo and Narongchai Akrasanee (Eds.), *The Future of Asia-Pacific Economics: Emerging Role of Asian NIES and ASEAN: Papers and Proceedings of the Conference held in November 1989 in Bangkok* (New Delhi: Allied Publishers, 1992), pp. 155-210.

- INFRASTRUCTURAL ECONOMY

383 Gao, Xinmin. 'China's Information Service Infrastructure and Its Strategy for Growth', in N. Seshagiri, *et.al.* (Eds.), *Information Systems for Economies in Transition: Papers Presented at the International Conference, ISET-IC, March 4-7, 1996, Ghaziabad, India* (New Delhi: Tata McGraw-Hill Publishing Company, 1996), pp. 135-46.

- INTERNATIONAL ECONOMICS

-- Foreign Aid

384 Katoh, Yuzoh. 'A Review of Japanese Official Direct Assistance and Foreign Direct Investment to India', in *Proceedings of the Symposium on Role of Direct Cooperation in Promoting Economic Relations Between India, Germany, the EC, and Japan: Papers, Proceedings and Recommendations* (Bombay: Indian Merchants Chamber, 1992), pp. 37-41.

-- Foreign Investment

385 Adwant, Vijay Kumar. 'Impact of Foreign Direct Investment on India and China (1985-1990)', in B. Satyanarayan (Ed.), *A Comparative Study of Foreign Direct Investment in China and India* (Bombay: Himalaya Publishing House, 1996), pp. 114-18.

386 Chawla, R.L. 'Prospects of the Indo-Japan Investment Potential', in S.P. Gupta and R.L. Chawla (Eds.), *Prospects of Foreign Investment in India in Post-Liberalisation Era* (New Delhi: Indian Council for Research on International Economic Relations, 1995), pp. 119-26.

387 Gupta, I.D. 'Foreign Direct Investment in China and India: Planning and Direct Strategy', in B. Satyanarayan (Ed.), *A Comparative Study of Foreign Direct Investment in China and India* (Bombay: Himalaya Publishing House, 1996), pp. 25-38.

388 Indrakant, S. 'Impact on Foreign Direct Investment in India and China—An Empirical Analysis in China and India', in B. Satyanarayan (Ed.), *A Comparative Study of Foreign Direct Investment in China and India* (Bombay: Himalaya Publishing House, 1996), pp. 128-38.

389 Iqbal, Badar A. 'Japan's FDI Attaining New Heights', in Manjit Singh Narang (Ed.), *International Industries Annual, 1991* (Delhi: Manjit Singh Narang, 1992), pp. 285-89.

390 Jaikumar, R. 'China—The Foreign Investment Scenario (With Special Reference to Joint Ventures)', in Bibek Debroy (Ed.), *China's External Trade Since the Reforms*

(New Delhi: Commonwealth Publishers, 1991), pp. 330-48.

391 Jauhari, B.M. 'Present Strategy of Direct Investment in India and China', in B. Satyanarayan (Ed.), *A Comparative Study of Foreign Direct Investment in China and India* (Bombay: Himalaya Publishing House, 1996), pp. 198-207.

392 Kala, N. 'Globalization—Emerging Dimensions: Experiences of China and India', in B. Satyanarayan (Ed.), *A Comparative Study of Foreign Direct Investment in China and India* (Bombay: Himalaya Publishing House, 1996), pp. 152-64.

393 Kesavan, K.V. 'Japan's Investment Interest in India and Southeast Asia', in Sri Prakash, *et.al.* (Eds.), *India and ASEAN: Economic Partnership in the 1990s and Future Prospects* (New Delhi: Gyan Publishing House, 1996), pp. 97-101.

394 Lakshmi, S. 'Foreign Direct Investment—Aims, Policies and Trends in India and China', in B. Satyanarayan (Ed.), *A Comparative Study of Foreign Direct Investment in China and India* (Bombay: Himalaya Publishing House, 1996), pp. 228-34.

395 Mishra, S.N. and Goldar, B. *Japanese Direct Investment in India* (Delhi: Institute of Economic Growth, 1993), *Mimeograph.*

396 Murthy, Gautam. 'Foreign Direct Investment in LDCs: Trends in India and China', in B. Satyanarayan (Ed.), *A Comparative Study of Foreign Direct Investment in China and India* (Bombay: Himalaya Publishing House, 1996), pp. 55-65.

397 Prasad, P. 'Foreign Direct Investment and Direct', in B. Satyanarayan (Ed.), *A Comparative Study of Foreign Direct Investment in China and India* (Bombay: Himalaya Publishing House, 1996), pp. 220-27.

398 Ramakrishna, S. 'A Comparative Study of Investment Planning and Patterns for Foreign Direct Investment in India and China: Some Issues', in B. Satyanarayan (Ed.), *A Comparative Study of Foreign Direct Investment in China*

and India (Bombay: Himalaya Publishing House, 1996), pp. 66-81.

399 Rao, A.V.V.S.K. 'Foreign Direct Investment—Policy Responses: Trends in India and China', in B. Satyanarayan (Ed.), *A Comparative Study of Foreign Direct Investment in China and India* (Bombay: Himalaya Publishing House, 1996), pp. 119-27.

400 Rao, K. Chakradhar. 'Imperialism, FDI, India and China', in B. Satyanarayan (Ed.), *A Comparative Study of Foreign Direct Investment in China and India* (Bombay: Himalaya Publishing House, 1996), pp. 165-8.

401 Reddy, J. Mahender. 'Foreign Direct Investment in China and India', in B. Satyanarayan (Ed.), *A Comparative Study of Foreign Direct Investment in China and India* (Bombay: Himalaya Publishing House, 1996), pp. 1-13.

402 Roy, Lipi. 'Japan—Leading Investor in Asia-Pacific', in Lipi Roy, *Foreign Direct Investment: Status and Prospects* (New Delhi: Associated Chamber of Commerce and Industry of India, 1995), p. 10.

403 Saibaba, G. and Krishna, G.R. 'FDI in India and China: Trends and Issues', in B. Satyanarayan (Ed.), *A Comparative Study of Foreign Direct Investment in China and India* (Bombay: Himalaya Publishing House, 1996), pp. 208-19.

404 Satyanarayan, B. (Ed.), *A Comparative Study of Foreign Direct Investment in China and India* (Bombay: Himalaya Publishing House, 1996).

405 Shanmugasundaram, V. 'A Comparative Study of FDI in India and China: Problems and Perspectives', in B. Satyanarayan (Ed.), *A Comparative Study of Foreign Direct Investment in China and India* (Bombay: Himalaya Publishing House, 1996), pp. 235-38.

406 Sudesh. 'Foreign Direct Investment in India Vis-a-Vis China', in R.K. Tandon and S.L. Gupta (Eds.), *Globalization of Indian Financial Markets* (New Delhi: Anmol Publications, 1995), pp. 195-204.

407 Zaidi, Naseem A. 'Foreign Direct Investment in India and China', in B. Satyanarayan (Ed.), *A Comparative*

Study of Foreign Direct Investment in China and India (Bombay: Himalaya Publishing House, 1996), pp. 14-24.

-- Foreign Trade

408 'Agreement Between India and China on Trade and Intercourse Between Tibet Region of China and India, April 29, 1954', in S.C. Bhatt, *The Triangle, India-Nepal-China: A Study of Treaty Relations* (New Delhi: Gyan Publishing House, 1996), pp. 275-82.

409 'Agreement on Trade, Intercourse and Related Questions Between Tibet and Autonomous Region of China and Nepal, May 2, 1966', in S.C. Bhatt, *The Triangle, India-Nepal-China: A Study of Treaty Relations* (New Delhi: Gyan Publishing House, 1996), pp. 314-18.

410 Anil Kumar (Ed.), 'China' and 'Japan', in Anil Kumar (Ed.), *World Importers Directory* (Delhi: Anupam Publications, 1996), pp. 296-98 and 810-93.

411 Banerjee, Brojendra Nath. 'China's Re-entry to GATT', in Brojendra Nath Banerjee, *Multinational Scramble for New Markets: WTO, Dunkel, GATT* (New Delhi: New Age International, 1996), pp. 246-75.

412 Banerjee, Brojendra Nath. 'Sino-Indian Comparison', in Brojendra Nath Banerjee, *Multinational Scramble for New Markets: WTO, Dunkel, GATT* (New Delhi: New Age International, 1996), pp. 265-68.

413 Behl, Ramesh and Mago, L.D. 'External Trade of China', in Bibek Debroy (Ed.), *China's External Trade Since the Reforms* (New Delhi: Commonwealth Publishers, 1991), pp. 74-224.

414 Behl, Ramesh and Mago, L.D. Sino-Indian Trade', in Bibek Debroy (Ed.), *China's External Trade Since the Reforms* (New Delhi: Commonwealth Publishers, 1991), pp. 263-91.

415 Bhattacharyya, B. and Sengupta, A.K. 'Country Profiles: Hong Kong', in B. Bhattacharyya and A.K. Sengupta, *Exporters Handbook: Strategic Information and Intelligence* (New Delhi: Indian Institute of Foreign Trade; Global Business Press, 1996), pp. 205-11.

416 Bhattacharyya, B. and Sengupta, A.K. 'Country Profiles: Japan', in B. Bhattacharyya and A.K. Sengupta, *Exporters Handbook: Strategic Information and Intelligence* (New Delhi: Indian Institute of Foreign Trade; Global Business Press, 1996), pp. 146-216.

417 'China, Taiwan, Hong Kong, Japan', in Marine Products Export Development Authority, *Statistics of Marine Products Export, 1991* (Cochin: Marine Products Export Development Authority, 1992), pp. 48-50.

418 'China, Taiwan, Hong Kong, Japan', in Marine Products Export Development Authority, *Statistics of Marine Products Export, 1992* (Cochin: Marine Products Export Development Authority, 1993), pp. 68-70.

419 'China, Taiwan, Hong Kong, Japan', in Marine Products Export Development Authority, *Statistics of Marine Products Export, 1993* (Cochin: Marine Products Export Development Authority, 1994), pp. 26-30.

420 Debroy, Bibek. 'Chinese Counter-Trade Practice', in Bibek Debroy (Ed.), *China's External Trade Since the Reforms* (New Delhi: Commonwealth Publishers, 1991), pp. 292-305.

421 Debroy, Bibek. (Ed.), *China's External Trade Since the Reforms* (New Delhi: Commonwealth Publishers, 1991).

422 'Foreign Importers: Japan', in R.L. Bhalla (Ed.), *Directory of International Importers* (Delhi: Directory of International Importers, 1995), pp. 147-89.

423 Government of India, Ministry of Mines, Indian Bureau of Mines. 'Foreign Markets: China Japan', in *Manganese Ore: A Market Survey* (Nagpur: Controller General, Indian Bureau of Mines, 1995), pp. 29, 34.

424 Holliman, Jonathan. 'Japan's Trade in Tropical Timber with South East Asia', in Vandana Shiva, *et.al.*, *Foreign Resources: Crisis and Management* (Dehra Dun: Natraj Publishers, 1992), pp. 250-59.

425 Huang, Danhan. 'China's Foreign Trade System and its Ongoing Reform', in S.P. Gupta, *et.al.* (Eds.), *Development Patterns and Institutional Structures: China and India* (New Delhi: Allied Publishers, 1995), pp. 257-74.

426 Iqbal, B.A. *India's Trade with Japan: Performance and Prospects* (New Delhi: Academic Foundation, 1990) .

427 'Itemwise Exports to East Asia', in *Handbook of Export Statistics, 1991, 1992, 1993-94* (New Delhi: Apparel Export Promotion Council, 1994), pp. 181-90.

428 'Japan', in *Directory of Importers of Marine Products* (Kochi: Marine Products Exports Development Authority, 1993), pp. 73-106.

429 Kezoka, Frank. 'How to Sell a Product to the Japanese Market', in B. Krishnamoorthi, *et.al.* (Eds.), *Proceedings of the Seminar on Fisheries: A Multibillion Dollar Industry, Held at Madras From August 17 to 19, 1995* (Madras: Aquaculture Foundation of India, 1996), pp. 153-54.

430 Koshy, Darlie O. 'The Japanese Clothing Market', in *Effective Export Marketing of Apparel to the US, EU and Japan* (Delhi: Global Business Press, 1995), pp. 164-91.

431 Kotler, P. 'Japan's Success in Global Marketing', in P.R. Shukla and S.K. Roy Chowdhry (Eds.), *International Trade, Finance, Market and India's Exports* (New Delhi: Akashdeep Publishing House, 1992), pp. 347-79.

432 Madan Lal. 'China: Reintegration into GATT', in Bibek Debroy (Ed.), *China's External Trade Since the Reforms* (New Delhi: Commonwealth Publishers, 1991), pp. 383-411.

433 Moitra, M.C. 'China Teas', in M.C. Moitra, *New Dimension of Tea: Its Projection in the 21st Century* (Howrah, M.C. Moitra, 1991), pp. 148-50.

434 Nandakumar, T. 'China', in T. Nandakumar, *Directory of Tariff/Non-Tariff Restructuring on Spice Trade* (Cochin: Spices Board, Government of India, Ministry of Commerce, 1991), pp. 23-24.

435 Nandakumar, T. 'Japan', in T. Nandakumar, *Directory of Tariff/Non-Tariff Restructuring on Spice Trade* (Cochin: Spices Board, Government of India, Ministry of Commerce, 1991), pp. 50-52.

436 Parthasarthy, N. 'Implications of Thaw in Sino-soviet Relations on India's Exports', in Bibek Debroy (Ed.),

China's External Trade Since the Reforms (New Delhi: Commonwealth Publishers, 1991), pp. 225-62.

437 Sri Prakash. 'The Political Economy of China's Trade With the Third World: A Micro Perspective for the 1990's', in Ausaf Ahmad, *Development Issues of the Third World* (New Delhi: Khanna Publishers, 1966), pp. 154-81.

438 'Trade and Economic Cooperation: People's Republic of China', in V. Vithal Babu (Ed.), *Trade and Technology Directory of India* (New Delhi: Economy and Trade, 1991), pp. 668-69.

-- Tourist Trade

439 Swain, Margaret Bryne. 'Ethnic Tourism Development in Yunnan, China: Shilin Sani', in Tej Vir Singh, *et.al. Tourism and Environment: Nature, Culture, Economy* (New Delhi: Inter-India Publications, 1992), pp. 172-82.

- INTERNATIONAL ECONOMIC RELATIONS

-- China-Asean

440 Sri Prakash. 'China-ASEAN: Economic Relations', in Sri Prakash, *et.al.* (Eds.), *India and ASEAN: Economic Partnership in the 1990s and Future Prospects* (New Delhi: Gyan Publishing House, 1996), pp. 157-213.

-- China-India

441 Madan Lal. 'China', in Manjit Singh Narang (Ed.), *International Industries Annual 1991* (New Delhi: Manjit Singh Narang, 1992), pp. 349-55.

442 Singh, Awadhesh Kumar. 'Sino-Indian Relations: Prospects for Trade', in G.S. Batra and Narinder Kaur (Eds.), *Management of Economic Crisis* (New Delhi: Anmol Publications, 1995), pp. 1-30 .

-- China-World

443 Pu, Shan. 'Vision of the Asia-Pacific Region: China's Econnomic Outlook and Policies in Response to Ongoing Global Adjustments', in Fu-chen Lo and Narongchai Akrasanee (Eds.), *The Future of Asia-Pacific Economics: Emerging Role of Asian NIES and ASEAN: Papers and*

Proceedings of the Conference held in November 1989 in Bangkok (New Delhi: Allied Publishers, 1992), pp. 43-46.

-- China-Japan

444 Gurumurthi, S. 'China', in *Development Through Aid: Role of Japan* (New Delhi: Vikas Publishing House, 1996), pp. 44-61.

-- Hong Kong-India

445 Behl, Ramesh and Mago, L.D. 'Hong Kong', in Ramesh Behl and L.D. Mago, *India's Major Trading Partners: Profiles* (New Delhi: Indian Institute of Foreign Trade, 1995), pp. 103-44.

-- Japan - Asia, East: China

446 Jain, R.K. 'Sino-Japanese Economic Relations', in C.S. Nagpal and A.C. Mittal (Eds.), *A Comparative Study in International Trade* (New Delhi: Anmol Publications, 1993), pp. 376-98.

-- Japan - Asia, South

447 Esho, Hideki. 'Japanese Investment in South Asia: The Case of India', in Purnendra Jain, *Distant Asian Neighbours: Japan and South Asia* (New Delhi: Sterling Publishers, 1996), pp. 64-84.

448 Gupta, S.P., *et.al.* (Eds.) *Cooperation for Growth: Perspective on Japan-South Asia Relations* (New Delhi: Macmillan, 1994).

-- India

449 Behl, Ramesh and Mago, L.D. 'Japan', in Ramesh Behl and L.D. Mago, *India's Major Trading Partners: Profiles* (New Delhi: Indian Institute of Foreign Trade, 1995), pp. 174-207.

450 Gurumurthi, S. *Development Through Aid: Role of Japan* (New Delhi: Vikas Publishing House, 1996).

451 Iqbal, Badar Alam. 'Japan's Economic Cold War with the U.S.', in Manjit Singh Narang (Ed.), *International Studies Annual, 1994* (New Delhi: Manjit Singh Narang, 1995), pp. 49-51.

452 Jain, Purnendra and Todhunter, Maureen. 'India and Japan: Newly Tempering Relations', in Purnendra Jain, *Distant Asian Neighbours: Japan and South Asia* (New Delhi: Sterling Publishers, 1996), pp. 85-107.

453 Kanwar, Kamlendra (Ed.). *India-Japan: Towards a New Era* (New Delhi: UBS Publishers' Distributors, 1992).

454 Kesavan, K.V. 'Japan, India and the EC: An Analysis of Their Economic Interaction', in K.B. Lall, *et.al.*, *India, Germany, and the European Community* (New Delhi: Radiant Publishers, 1993), pp. 92-98.

455 Krishnaswami, N. 'India and Japan: Removing Mental Blocks', in N. Krishnaswami, *Know Japan, Know the Japanese* (Madras: T.R. Publications, 1996), pp. 91-96.

456 Leonard, A.G. *India's Trade Relations with Japan: An Economic Analysis* (New Delhi: Indus Publishing Company, 1993).

457 Mishra, Ranjan Kumar. 'India and the Japanese Enigma', in Ranjan Kumar Mishra, *India and International Relations* (New Delhi: Kanishka Publishers Distributors, 1996), pp. 131-60.

458 Naqvi, S.N.H. 'Prospects of Economic Collaboration Between Japan and South Asia' in S.P. Gupta, *et.al.* (Eds.), *Cooperation For Change* (New Delhi: Macmillan, 1994), pp. 37-47.

459 Narasimha Murthy, P.A. *India and Japan: Dimensions of Their Relations: Economic and Cultural* (New Delhi: Lancers Books, 1993).

460 Oppenlaender, Karl H. *Development Cooperation for Strengthening International Economic Relations: India, Germany, EC and Japan* (New Delhi: Indian Council for Research on International Economic Relations, 1992).

461 Venkataramini, R. *Japan Enters Indian Industry* (New Delhi: Radiant Publishers, 1990).

462 Vithal Babu, V. 'Trade and Economic Cooperation: Japan', in V. Vithal Babu, *Trade and Technology Directory of India* (New Delhi: Economy and Trade, 1991), pp. 679-80.

—

463 Vittal, N. 'Doing Business With Japan', in N. Vittal, *The Vicious Cycle of Vittal's Law* (New Delhi: Vikas, 1994), pp. 172-80.

464 Yamada, Chusei. 'Prospects for Indo-Japanese Economic Cooperation under Liberalized Policy', in Ashok V. Bhuleshkar and Suresh R. Desai (Eds.), *Indian Economy Under Liberalised System—Issues and Problems* (Bombay: Himalaya Publishing House, 1995), pp. 191-96.

465 Yoo, Jung-Ho. 'Trilateral Trade Relations Among Asian NIES, the US and Japan', in Fu-chen Lo and Narongchai Akrasanee (Eds.), *The Future of Asia-Pacific Economics: Emerging Role of Asian NIES and ASEAN: Papers and Proceedings of the Conference held in November 1989 in Bangkok* (New Delhi: Allied Publishers, 1992), pp. 211-45.

-- Japan - Asia, South East

466 Nagesh, Narayana. *Japan's Economic Diplomacy in Southeast Asia* (New Delhi: Lancers Books, 1996).

-- Japan - World

467 Chaitanya, Rachna. 'The New Hegemon—Japan', in Rachna Chaitanya. *The New World Order* (New Delhi: Radiant Publishers, 1995), pp. 35-68.

468 Higuchi, Yasuko. The Campaign Against 3rd World Forest Resources Exploitation by Japan', in Vandana Shiva, *et.al.*, *Forest Resources: Crisis and Management* (Dehra Dun: Natraj Publishers, 1992), pp. 360-70.

469 Varma, Lalima. 'Japan's Role in a Changing World', in Alokesh Barua, *Global Order, Recent Changes and Responses* (New Delhi: Lancers Books, 1992), pp. 156-65.

- JOINT VENTURES/MULTINATIONALS

470 Shiva Ramu, S. 'Multinationals: Chinese Multinationals', in S. Shiva Ramu, *The Dragons of Asia: Asia-Pacific Rim Countries and Their Multinations* (New Delhi: A.H. Wheeler and Company, 1995), pp. 183-95.

471 Shiva Ramu, S. 'Multinationals of Hong Kong', in S. Shiva Ramu, *The Dragons of Asia: Asia-Pacific Rim Countries and Their Multinationals* (New Delhi: A.H. Wheeler and Company, 1995), pp. 210-26.

472 Shiva Ramu, S. 'Multinationals of Taiwan', in S. Shiva Ramu, *The Dragons of Asia: Asia-Pacific Rim Countries and Their Multinationals* (New Delhi: A.H. Wheeler and Company, 1995), pp. 227-35.

473 Wilpert, Bernhard. 'Inter-cultural Management: Joint Ventures in the People's Republic of China', in Henry S.R. Rao *et.al.*, (Eds.), *Effective Organizations and Social Values* (New Delhi: Sage Publications, 1994), pp. 85-99.

- LABOUR AND LABOUR PROBLEMS

474 Ge, Man. 'Developing Social Security Systems in China', in T.S. Sankaran, *et.al.* (Eds.), *Social Security in Developing Countries* (New Delhi: Har-Anand Publications, 1994), pp. 138-50.

475 Jaspal Singh. 'Industrial Relations in Germany and Japan', in Jaspal Singh, *Contributions to Industrial Sociology* (New Delhi: National Book Organisation, 1991), pp. 38-42.

476 Jaspal Singh. 'The Japanese Model', in Jaspal Singh, *Contributions to Industrial Sociology* (New Delhi: National Book Organisation, 1991), pp. 43-47.

477 Thakur, Devendra and Aslam, Mahfooze. 'Measurement of Labour Productivity—The Japanese Experience', in Devendra Thakur and Aslam Mahfooze (Eds.), *Quantitative Techniques in Production and Productivity* (New Delhi: Deep and Deep Publications, 1996), pp. 232-37.

478 Zhang, Jianxin. 'Introduction to Social Security System in China', in T.S. Sankaran, *et.al.* (Eds.), *Social Security in Developing Countries* (New Delhi: Har-Anand Publications, 1994), pp. 151-62.

479 Pan, Feng and Li, Xi-Zheng. 'Developing a System for Integrating Planned Economy with Market Regulation in China: Some Labour Market Perspectives', in M. Mugtada and A. Hildeman (Eds.), *Labour Markets and Human Resource Planning in Asia: Perspectives and Evidence* (New Delhi: UNDP; Asian Regional Team for Employment Promotion, 1993), pp. 234-42.

- MARKET ECONOMY

480 He, Raifeng. 'China's Socialist Market Economy', in Baidyanath Misra, *et.al.* (Eds.), *Socialism and Market Economy (Proceedings of Seminar on Socialism and Market Economy* (Meerut: Anu Books, 1996), pp. 114-19.

481 Liu, Zhaodong. 'The New Orientation of the Scientech Information as a Follow-up to the Transition to Market Economy: The Case of China', in N. Seshagiri, *et.al.* (Eds.), *Information Systems For Economies in Transition: Papers Presented at the International Conference, ISET-IC, March 4-7, 1996, Ghaziabad, India* (New Delhi: Tata McGraw-Hill Publishing Company, 1996), pp. 228-34.

- MINES AND MINERALS

482 Fujita, Minoru. 'Mining Activity of Japan', in Ajoy K. Ghose (Ed.), *Small-Scale Mining: A Global Overview* (Calcutta: Mining, Geological and Metallurgical Institute of India, 1994), pp. 133-40.

- PRIVATISATION AND LIBERALISATION

483 Ahluwalia, Isher Judge. 'Economic Liberalisation: Lessons from China', in Raj Kapila and Uma Kapila (Eds.), *Understanding India's Economic Reforms: The Past, the Present and the Future* (Delhi: Academic Foundation, 1995), Vol. 4, pp. 247-52.

484 'The Individual and Private Economy of China', in Chakradhari Aggarwal (Ed.), *SMEs Towards 2000: A Collection of Papers Presented at the 6th International Conference of Small Medium Enterprises Held at Seoul in April 1992 and the World Conference of Small and Medium Enterprises Held at Beijing in March 1993* (New Delhi: World Assembly of Small and Medium Enterprises, 1993), pp. 252-56.

- PUBLIC SECTOR

485 Raghavan, S.N. 'Recent Policy Reforms: The Japanese Experience', in S.N. Raghavan, *Public Sector in India: Changing Perspectives* (New Delhi: Asian Institute of Transport Development, 1994), pp. 133-34.

486 Raghavan, S.N. 'Measures for Improving the Efficiency of Public Enterprises: The Chinese Experience', in

S.N. Raghavan, *Public Sector in India: Changing Perspectives* (New Delhi: Asian Institute of Transport Development, 1994), pp. 68-71.

487 Wang, Jun. 'Reforms of Public Enterprises in China', in S.L. Rao (Ed.), *Reforming State-owned Enterprises* (New Delhi: National Council of Applied Economic Research, 1996), pp. 5-36.

- REGIONAL ECONOMY

488 Shu, Shangzi. Some Questions of the Third World Economic Development by Example of the South-West Region of China', in R. Sharma (Ed.), *Regional Policies and Development in the Third World* (Varanasi: Rishi Publications, 1994), pp. 197-201.

- SPECIAL ECONOMIC ZONES

489 Bahl, S.K. 'China's Economic and Technological Development Zones (ETDZs)', in S.P. Gupta, *Chinese Economic Reforms* (New Delhi: Allied Publishers, 1996), pp. 75-127.

490 Devendra Prakash. 'Foreign Capital and Special Economic Zones', in Bibek Debroy (Ed.), *China's External Trade Since the Reforms* (New Delhi: Commonwealth Publishers, 1991), pp. 306-29.

491 Gao, Gwanjiang and Long, Guo Qiang. 'Special Economic Zones (SEZ) and Economic and Technological Development Zones (ETDZ) in China', in S.P. Gupta (Ed.), *China's Economic Reforms: The Role of Special Economic Zones and Technological Development Zones* (New Delhi: Allied Publishers, 1996), pp. 129-67.

492 Gupta, S.P. (Ed.), China's Economic Reforms*: The Role of Special Economic Zones and Technological Development Zones* (New Delhi: Allied Publishers, 1996).

493 Hameed, Shalul. 'China's Special Economic Zones', in S.P. Gupta (Ed.), *China's Economic Reforms: The Role of Special Economic Zones and Technological Development Zones* (New Delhi: Allied Publishers, 1996), pp. 33-73.

494 Kundra, Ashok. 'EPZs/EOU of India: Relevance of China's Experience', in S.P. Gupta (Ed.), *China's*

Economic Reforms: The Role of Special Economic Zones and Technological Development Zones (New Delhi: Allied Publishers, 1996), pp. 169-212.

EDUCATION

- ADMINISTRATION AND MANAGEMENT

495 Nachchattar Singh (Ed.). 'The Dilemma of Organisational Paralysis: A Case Profile From Japanese Academia', in Nachchattar Singh, *Readings in Organizational Behaviour* (New Delhi: APH Publishers, 1997), Vol. I, pp. 295-330.

496 Nigam, B.K. and Sharma, S.R. 'Educational System in China', in B.K. Nigam and S.R. Sharma (Eds.), *Principles and Methods of Comparative Educational System* (Delhi: Kanishka Publishers' Distributors, 1993), pp. 240-87.

497 Nigam, B.K. and Sharma, S.R. 'Educational System in Japan', in B.K. Nigam and S.R. Sharma (Eds.), *Principles and Methods of Comparative Educational System* (Delhi: Kanishka Publishers' Distributors, 1993), pp. 288-317.

- ADULT EDUCATION

498 Bhat, Seva Suman. 'The Anti-Illiteracy Campaigns in the People's Republic of China From 1950 to 1980', in Seva Suman Bhat, *Growth and Development of Adult Education* (New Delhi: Cosmo Publications, 1992), pp. 171-75.

499 Chakrabarti, Sreemati. 'Women and Adult Literacy in China: A Preliminary Enquiry', in Rajesh (Ed.), *Non-Formal Education: A Comparative Study* (Delhi: B.R. Publishing Cormporation, 1996), pp. 15-40.

500 Rao, Digumarti Bhaskara (Ed.). 'China', in Digumarti Bhaskara Rao (Ed.), *Education For All: Encyclopedia of Education for All* (New Delhi: APH Publishing Corporation, 1996), Vol. 2, pp. 93-99.

501 Shirur, Rajani R. 'China', in Rajani R. Shirur, *Experiences of Selected Third World Countries in Adult Literacy* (Calcutta: New Central Book Agency, 1992), pp. 137-50.

502 University of Delhi, Teaching Materials Development DACEE. 'Open Learning System for Hong Kong: Problems and Possibilities', in Rajesh (Ed.), *Non-Formal*

Education: A Comparative Study (Delhi: B.R. Publishing Corporation, 1996), pp. 141-52.

503 Vishwanathan, Savitri. 'Non-Formal Education in Japan', in Rajesh (Ed.), *Non-Formal Education: A Comparative Study* (Delhi: B.R. Publishing Cornporation, 1996), pp. 9-14.

504 Wang, Yianwei. 'Reform in Literacy Education in China', in A.L. Rahi (Ed.), *Adult Education: Trends and Issues* (Ambala Cantt: Indian Publications, 1994), pp. 336-45.

- CHRISTIAN EDUCATION

505 Chiang, Mao-Sing. 'An Evaluation of the Theological Curriculum of China Lutheran Seminary: From the Perspective of its Alumni', in Edith Woods (Ed.), *Education That Transforms: Perspectives in Christian Education in Asia* (Bangalore: Book Trust, 1995), pp. 223-24.

506 Giok, Wanda Po, Liam. 'Filial Piety in China's Culture and Christian Education', in Edith Woods (Ed.), *Education That Transforms: Perspectives in Christian Education in Asia* (Bangalore: Bangalore Book Trust, 1995), pp. 203-20.

- ELEMENTARY/SCHOOL EDUCATION

507 Sharma, Shobha. 'Survey of Promoting Children's Education in Malaysia, Thailand and Japan', in Ajay Kumar Sharma (Ed.), *Advances in Library and Information Sciences* (Modinagar: Library Progress, 1994), pp. 5-8.

- HIGHER EDUCATION

508 Biswas, A. 'Education in China and Japan', in A. Biswas, *Comparative Education: India, UK, USA, USSR, Russian Federation, China and Japan* (New Delhi: Arya Book Depot, 1995), pp. 319-43.

- PHYSICAL EDUCATION

509 Tagore, Rabindranath. 'Takagaki', in Rabindranath Tagore, *The English Writings of Rabindranath Tagore*: ed. by Sisir Kumar Das (New Delhi: Sahitya Akademi, 1996), Vol. 3: A miscellany, pp. 795-96.

- PROFESSIONAL EDUCATION

510 Um, Young Ai. 'Library Education in Japan, the Republic of Korea and Taiwan: A Comparative Study', in Paramjit Singh Kwatra (Ed.), *World Encyclopaedia of Library and Information Science Education* (New Delhi: Crest Publishing House, 1994), pp. 171-89.

511 Xinxia, Lai. 'Education for Library and Information Science and its Future in China', in Paramjit Singh Kwatra (Ed.), *World Encyclopaedia of Library and Information Science Education* (New Delhi: Crest Publishing House, 1994), pp. 159-70.

- STUDY AND TEACHING

512 Mayeda, Sengaku. 'Indian Studies in Japan: Retrospect and Prospect', in K. Satchidananda Murthy and Amit Dasgupta (Eds.), *The Perennial Tree: Select Papers of the International Symposium on Indian Studies* (New Delhi: Indian Council for Cultural Relations, New Age International, 1996), pp. 108-22.

513 Tara, Masanoba. 'The History of Science Education in Japan: 1860-1978', in V.K. Gupta (Ed.), *Science and Technology Education: New Thrusts and Recent Trends* (Chandigarh: Arun Publishing House, 1996), pp. 426-77.

514 Zhao, Xueshu. 'STS Education of Secondary Science Education in China', in V.K. Gupta (Ed.), *Science and Technology Education: New Thrusts and Recent Trends* (Chandigarh: Arun Publishing House, 1996), pp. 75-86.

GEOGRAPHY

- CLIMATOLOGY

515 Zhai, Yongping. 'Challenges of CO_2 Abatement in China: What Measures and What Targets', in L.M. Saxena and Vinod Gupta (Eds.), *Global Warming and Atmospheric Change* (Delhi: Indian Environmental Society, 1992), pp. 37-51.

516 Mukherjee, B.N. 'Earliest Datable Routes for North-Eastern India's Communication with China and South-East Asia in the Historical Period', in B.N. Mukherjee,

External Trade of Early North-Eastern India (New Delhi: Har-Anand Publications, 1992), pp. 17-29.

- HISTORICAL

517 Chamaria, Pradeep. 'Tibet', in Pradeep Chamaria, *Kailash Manasarovar: On the Rugged Road to Revelation* (New Delhi: Abhinav Publications, 1996), pp. 75-84.

518 Dyhrenfurth, G.O. 'History of Expeditions on the Tibetan Side', in G.D. Dyhrenfurth and Erwin Schneider. *To The Third Pole: The History of the High Himalaya* (New Delhi: Cosmo Publications, 1994).

519 Liu, Xinru. *Silk and Religion: An Exploration of Material Life and the Thought of People, AD 600-1200* (Delhi: Oxford University Press, 1996).

- PHYSICAL

520 Hill, R.D. 'A People-Land 'Crunch': Guizhou Province, P.R.C.', in R.B. Singh (Ed.), *Research in Geography* (New Delhi: APH Publishing Corporation, 1996), Vol. 1, pp. 255-69.

520A Leckie, Scott. *The Urban Fate of Lhasa: Destruction of an Ancient Habitat* (Dharamsala: Central Tibetan Administration, Department of Information and International Relations, 1996).

521 Zhu, Daiqiang. 'East Asia: Islands in Chinese Territorial Claims', in Garry Trompf (Ed.), *Islands and Enclaves: Nationalisms and Separatist Pressures in Island and Littoral Contexts* (New Delhi: Sterling, 1993), pp. 175-92.

- TRAVEL AND DESCRIPTION

522 Ahir, D.C. 'Chinese Pilgrims in Buddha Gaya', in D.C. Ahir, *Buddha Gaya Through the Ages* (Delhi: Sri Satguru Publications, 1994), pp. 35-53.

523 Aswal, Devender Singh. *From Central Hall to the Great Hall* (Ghaziabad: K.L. Sharma, 1993).

524 Chopra, S.N. *China Today: An Overview of People's Republic* (Delhi: Konark Publishers, 1993).

- URBAN

525 Tsomo, Tsering. *Urban Morphology of Lhasa, Tibet* (New Delhi: Intellectual Publishing House, 1994).

526 Himiyama, Yukio and Jitsu, Kiyotaka, 'Recent Achievements in Land Use Studies in Japan', in R.B. Singh (Ed.), *Research in Geography* (New Delhi: APH Publishing Corporation, 1996), Vol. 1, pp. 31-46.

527 Sengupta, Sukumar. 'Medical Science as Known to the Chinese Pilgrims', in P.K. Mishra (Ed.), *Aspects of Indian History and Historiography: Professor Kalyan Kumar Dasgupta Felicitation Volume* (New Delhi: Kaveri Books, 1996), pp. 173-77.

528 Sarabhai, Mrinali. 'Remembering My Visit to China', in Tan Chung (Ed.), *China and India* (New Delhi: Indian Council for Cultural Relations, 1994), pp. 477-81; *Indian Horizons*, Special Issue, Vol. 43, Nos. 1-2, 1994.

529 Sen, Kshitimohan. 'Meetings of Brothers: With Gurudeva in China', in Tan Chung (Ed.), *China and India* (New Delhi: Indian Council for Cultural Relations, 1994), pp. 75-83; *Indian Horizons*, Special Issue, Vol. 43, Nos. 1-2, 1994.

530 Matsuda, Iware. 'Natural Disasters and Counter-Measures For the Tokyo Lowland', in R.B. Singh (Ed.), *Research in Geography* (New Delhi: APH Publishing Corporation, 1996), Vol. 2, pp. 91-104.

531 Nishikawa, Osamu. 'Challenge and Response in the Relationship Between Typhoon Disasters and Human Action in Japan', in R.B. Singh (Ed.), *Research in Geography* (New Delhi: APH Publishing Corporation, 1996), Vol. 2, pp. 125-42.

532 Chandrasekharan, S. 'Dr. Radhakrishnan's China Visit in 1944', in Tan Chung (Ed.), *China and India* (New Delhi: Indian Council for Cultural Relations, 1994), pp. 459-68; *Indian Horizons*, Special Issue, Vol. 43, Nos. 1-2, 1994.

HISTORY

- ANCIENT

533 Choudhury, Paramesh. *Northeast, The Cradle of the Chinese Nation* (Calcutta: P. Choudhury, 1995).

534 Gupta, Murari Lal. *A Short History of China: Since Ancient Times Till 1992* (New Delhi: Reliance Publishing House, 1994).

535 Hassnain, F.M. *Kashgar—Central Asia* (New Delhi: Reliance Publishing House, 1995).

536 Kulkarni, S.D. 'India and China', in S.D. Kulkarni, *India Abroad* (Bombay: Shri Bhagavan Vedavyasa Itihasa Samshodhana Mandira, Bhishma, 1995), pp. 27-35.

537 Kulkarni, S.D. 'Tibet', in S.D. Kulkarni, *India Abroad* (Bombay: Shri Bhagavan Vedavyasa Itihasa Samshodhana Mandira, Bhishma, 1995), pp. 36-38.

538 Kuppuswami, T.V. 'Embassies to China', in S.D. Kulkarni (Ed.), *History of Tamilakam* (Bombay: Shri Bhagavan Vedavyasa Itihasa Samshodhana Mandira Bhishma, 1995); *Bhishma's Study of Indian History and Culture*, Vol. 5, pts. 1-2, pp. 270-71.

539 Lokesh Chandra. 'Emperor Hsuan-Tsung, Vajrayana and Quarter of Vajras', in Lokesh Chandra, *Cultural Heritage of India* (New Delhi: International Academy of Indian Culture, Aditya Prakashan, 1992), Vol. 2, pp. 267-76.

540 Misra, Satya Swarup. 'Evidence of Indo-Aryan Contact With Chinese and Korean in 2nd-3rd Millennium BC', in Satya Swarup Misra, *The Aryan Problem: A Linguistic Approach* (New Delhi: Munshiram Manoharlal Publishers, 1992), pp. 53-55.

540A *The Mongols and Tibet: A Historical Assessment of Relations Between the Mongol Empire and Tibet* (Dharamsala: Central Tibetan Administration, Department of Information and International Relations, 1996).

541 Mukherjee, B.N. 'Kharoshti Inscriptions in the Kingdom of Shan-shan', in B.N. Mukherjee, *India in Early Central Asia: A Survey of Indian Scripts, Languages and Literatures in Central Asia of the First Millennium A.D.* (New Delhi: Harman Publishing House, 1996), pp. 38-65.

542 Mukherjee, B.N. 'A List of Dates in the Kharoshti Inscriptions of Shan-shan', in B.N. Mukherjee, *India in Early Central Asia: A Survey of Indian Scripts, Languages*

and Literatures in Central Asia of the First Millennium A.D. (New Delhi: Harman Publishing House, 1996), pp. 97-110.

543 Mukherjee, B.N. 'Shan-shan and the Kushana Empire', in B.N. Mukherjee, *India in Early Central Asia: A Survey of Indian Scripts, Languages and Literatures in Central Asia of the First Millennium A.D.* (New Delhi: Harman Publishing House, 1996), pp. 90-96.

544 Ramadas. 'Ruthless Secularism of a Chinese Autocrat', in Ramadas, *Is There Justice in Life*? (Bombay: Bharatiya Vidya Bhawan, 1995), pp. 27-28.

545 Ray, Harprasad. 'Nature of Trade and Diplomacy Between India and China During Ancient and Medieval Periods', in *Proceedings of the Indian History Congress, 54th Session (1993), Mysore* (Delhi: Indian History Congress, 1994), pp. 754-56.

546 Richardson, H.E. 'Monuments of the Yarhung Dynasty', in Pratapaditya Pillai (Ed.), *On the Path to Void: Buddhist Art of the Tibetan Realm* (Mumbai: Marg Publications, 1996), pp. 26-45.

547 Sen, Tansen. 'Maritime Contacts Between China and the Cola Kingdom (A.D. 850-1279), in K.S. Mathew (Ed.), *Mariners, Merchants and Oceans: Studies in Maritime History* (New Delhi: Manohar Publishers and Distributors, 1995), pp. 25-41.

548 Subbarayalu, Y. 'Chinese Ceramics of Tamil Nadu and Kerala Coasts', in Himanshu Prabha Ray and Jean-Francois Salles (Eds.), *Tradition and Archaeology: Early Maritime Contacts in the Indian Ocean: Proceedings of the International Seminar, Techno-Archaeological Perspectives of Seafaring in the Indian Ocean, 4th Century B.C. - 15th Century A.D., New Delhi, February 28 - March 4, 1994* (New Delhi: Manohar Publishers and Distributors, 1996), pp. 109-14.

549 Subrahmaniam, N. 'Original Sources: Chinese', in N. Subrahmaniam (Ed.), *Original Sources for the History of Tamilnad: From the Beginning to A.D. 600* (Udumalpet: Ennes Publications, 1994), pp. 291-96.

- NUMISMATICS

550 Cribb, Joe. 'Chinese Coin Finds From South India and Sri Lanka', in K.K. Maheshwari and Biswajeet Rath (Eds.), *Numismatic Panorama: Essays in Memory of Late Shri S.M. Shukla* (New Delhi: Harman Publishing House, 1996), pp. 253-70.

- MEDIEVAL

551 Norbu, Dawa. 'Imperialism and Inner Asia 1775-1907: How British India and Imperial China Redefined the Status of Tibet', in K. Warikoo and Dawa Norbu (Eds.), *Ethnicity and Politics in Central Asia* (New Dehi: South Asian Publishers, 1992), pp. 21-54.

552 Pandian, M.S. 'Bohar (1550-1625): Record of His Visits to China', in *Indian History Congress Proceedings of the Indian History Congress, 54th Session, 1993, Mysore* (Delhi: Indian History Congress, 1994), pp. 757-58.

553 Raghava Varier, M.R. 'Trade Relations Between Kerala and China, 1200-1500', in Indian History Congress, *Proceedings of Indian History Congress, 51st Session, Calcutta, 1990* (New Delhi: Indian History Congress, 1991), pp. 690-98.

554 Ray, Haraprasad. Trade and Diplomacy in India-China Relations: A Study of Bengal During the Fifteenth Century (New Delhi: Radiant Publishers, 1993).

555 Warikoo, A. 'China and Central Asia: Review of Ching Policy in Xingiang, 1755-1884', in K. Warikoo and Dawa Norbu, *Ethnicity and Politics in Central Asia* (New Delhi: South Asian Publishers, 1992), pp. 2-20.

- MODERN

556 Bajracharya, Bhadra Ratna. 'Confrontation with Tibet and China', in Bhadra Ratna Bajracharya, *Bahadur Shah: The Regent of Nepal, 1785-1794 A.D.* (New Delhi: Anmol Publications, 1992), pp. 281-351.

557 Beri, K.K. 'The Japanese Occupation of South-east Asia and its Aftermath', in K.K. Beri, *History and Culture of South-East Asia: Modern* (New Delhi: Sterling Publishers, 1994), pp. 217-59.

558 Bharadwaj, A.N. 'Chinese Invasion of Tibet', in A.N. Bharadwaj, *Failures of the UNO* (Jammu: Jay Kay Publications, 1996), pp. 86-134.

559 Bhonsle, R.K. *The Japanese Offensive, 1941-43: An Analytical Study* (New Delhi: Himalayan Books, 1990).

560 Chen, Tiejidu. 'Historical Process of the Chinese Revolution: From 1911 to 1949', in Manoranjan Mohanty (Ed.), *Chinese Revolution: Comparative Perspectives on Transformation of Non-Western Societies* (Delhi: Ajanta Publications, 1992), pp. 33-64.

561 David, M.D. *The Making of Modern China* (Bombay: Himalaya Publishing House, 1993).

562 Dhillon, Mohinder Singh. 'Japan Must Tender An Apology', in Mohinder Singh Dhillon, *A Titan in the Andamans, Dr. Diwan Singh Kalepani: A Biography* (Chandigarh: Angad Publishers, 1994), p. 471.

563 Dong, Dignan. 'Indian Revolutionaries and the Neutrality of China, 1915-1917', in Sarva Daman Singh (Ed.), *Culture Through the Ages: Professor B.N. Puri Felicitation Volume* (Delhi: Agam Kala Prakashan, 1996), pp. 241-56.

564 Dutt, Gargi and Dutt, V.P. *China After Mao* (New Delhi: Vikas Publishing House, 1991).

565 Gupta, S.P. and Ramachandran, K.S. *History of Tibet* (New Delhi: Tibetan Parliamentary and Policy Research Centre in association with Har-Anand Publications, 1995).

566 Kaul, M.N. 'Conversations Between Gandhi, Chiang-Kai-Shek and Madam Chiang', in S.L. Shakdher (Ed.), *Thoughts and Reflections of M.N. Kaul* (New Delhi: National Publishing House, 1993), pp. 168-86.

567 Koyama, Kosuke. 'Forgiveness and Politics: Japanese Experience', in Kosuke Koyama, *Bread and Breath: Essays in Honour of Samuel Rayan, on the Occasion of His Seventeenth Birth Anniversary* (Anand: Gujarat Sahitya Prakashan, 1991), pp. 139-67.

568 Majumdar, Inakshi. 'The Route: A Study of the Trade Route Connecting the Frontier Trade Post of Kalimpong

With the Plains of Bengal and Lhasa (1865-1965), in K.L. Shrimali, *et.al.* (Eds.), *Proceedings of the Indian History Congress, 55th Session, Aligarh, 1994* (Delhi: Indian History Congress, 1995), pp. 630-38.

569 Nehru, Jawaharlal. 'China and Tibet', in S. Gopal (Ed.), *Selected Works of Jawaharlal Nehru: Second Series* (New Delhi: Jawaharlal Nehru Memorial Fund; Distributed by Oxford University Press, 1996), Vol. 18, pp. 471-80.

570 Nehru, Jawaharlal. 'China and Tibet', in S. Gopal (Ed.), *Selected Works of Jawaharlal Nehru: Second Series* (New Delhi: Jawaharlal Nehru Memorial Fund; Distributed by Oxford University Press, 1996), Vol. 19, pp. 651-53.

571 Ng, Chin-Keong. 'The Amoy Riots of 1852--Coolie, Emigration and Sino-British Relations', in K.S. Mathur (Ed.), *Mariners, Merchants and Oceans: Studies in Maritime History* (New Delhi: Manohar Publishers and Distributors, 1995), pp. 419-46.

572 Prasad, Rajindra. *Colonialism, Lumpenization, Revolution* (Delhi: Ajanta Books International, 1995), Vol. 1, Societies of Calcutta and Shanghai, 1850-1914 (To be completed in 2 Volumes).

573 Ram Rahul. *Modern Tibet* (New Delhi: Munshiram Manoharlal, 1992).

574 Ramalingam, P. 'Dalai Lama: The Spiritual Head Awarded A Noble Prize - 1935', in P. Ramalingam, *History Through Personalities: Footprints, Handprints and Fingerprints on the Sands of Time* (Mumbai: Bharatiya Vidya Bhawan, 1996), pp. 189-90.

575 Ramalingam, P. 'Hirohito: An Emperor with a Difference', in P. Ramalingam, *History Through Personalities: Footprints, Handprints and Fingerprints on the Sands of Time* (Mumbai: Bharatiya Vidya Bhawan, 1996), pp. 160-61.

576 Saha, Meghnad. 'The Renaissance of China', in Meghnad Saha, *Collected Works of Meghnad Saha*: edited by Santimay Chatterjee (Calcutta: Saha Institute of Nuclear Physics; Bombay: Orient Longman, 1993), Vol. 4, pp. 385-439.

577 Saksena, Shalini. 'Communist China in Transition', in *Indian History Congress proceedings of the Indian History Congress , 54th Session, 1993, Mysore* (Delhi: Indian History Congress, 1994), pp. 764-65.

578 Saksena, Shalini. *India, China, and the Revolution* (New Delhi: Anmol Publications, 1992).

579 Sareen, T.R. *Japan and the Indian National Army* (New Delhi: Mounto Publishing House, 1996).

580 Sareen, T.R. 'Japanese Policy Towards India', in T.R. Sareen, *Japan and the Indian National Army* (New Delhi: Mounto Publishing House, 1996), pp. 84-106.

581 Sharma, S.K. and Sharma, Usha. *Encyclopaedia of Tibet* (New Delhi: Anmol Publications, 1996), 7 Vols. -- Vol. 1: History and Geography of Tibet; Vol. 2: Travel and Memories of Tibet; Vol. 3: Society and Culture of Tibet; Vol. 4: Religious Heritage of Tibet; Vol. 5: Dalai Lama and Tibet; Vol. 6: India and Tibet; Vol. 7: Tibet and the World. "Collected articles; most previously published".

582 Tagore, Rabindranath, 'Tagore and Noguchi (Yone)', in Rabindranath Tagore, *The English Writings of Rabindranath Tagore;* ed. by Sisir Kumar Das (New Delhi: Sahitya Akademi, 1996), Vol. 3: A Miscellany, pp. 834-45.

582A Tan, Chung. 'Towards a Holistic Understanding of Chinese History', in Barun De, *et.al.* (Eds.), *Proceedings of the Indian History Congress, 56th Session, 1995, Rabindra Bharati University* (Calcutta: Firma KLM, 1996), pp. 793-812.

583 Yamaguchi, Ichiro. 'The Meiji Restoration and the Chinese Revolution', in Manoranjan Mohanty (Ed.), *Chinese Revolution* (Delhi: Ajanta Publications, 1992), pp. 187-99.

-- Medical Mission to China

584 Latiff, Danial. 'Remembering Dr. Kotnis and the Indian Medical Mission to China', in Tan Chung (Ed.), *India and China* (New Delhi: Indian Council for Cultural Relations, 1994), pp. 217-19; *Indian Horizons*: Special Issue, Vol. 43, Vols. 1-2, 1994.

585 Sadhu, Suvarna. 'He Who Did Not Come Back: Remembering the Son of India Who Died for China', in Tan Chung (Ed.), *India and China* (New Delhi: Indian Council for Cultural Relations, 1994), pp. 201-15; *Indian Horizons*: Special Issue, Vol. 43, Vols. 1-2, 1994.

586 Lin, Chenju. 'Friends in Need: Comradeship Between Chinese and Indians in Their Common Struggle in Modern History', in Tan Chung (Ed.), *India and China* (New Delhi: Indian Council for Cultural Relations, 1994), pp. 37-62; *Indian Horizons*: Special Issue, Vol. 43, Vols. 1-2, 1994.

587 Bose, Subhas Chandra. 'Congress Medical Mission to China: Bose's Public Statement and Appeal, 28 June 1938; Bose's Speech at University Institute Hall, 12 August 1938', in Subhas Chandra Bose, *Netaji Collected Works* (Delhi: Oxford University Press, 1995), Vol. 9, pp. 36-39.

-- Missionary History

588 Bernard, K.L. 'The Chinese in Kerala', in K.L. Bernard, *Flashes of Kerala History* (Cochin: K.L. Bernard, 1995), pp. 32-35.

- MILITARY HISTORY

589 Liu, Man-Houng. 'World Recession, Indian Opium and China's Opium War', in K.S. Mathew (Ed.), *Mariners, Merchants and Oceans: Studies in Maritime History* (New Delhi: Manohar Publishers and Distributors, 1995), pp. 385-417 .

590 Virk, D.S., *et.al. C.E.F.: The Chinese Expeditionary Force, 1900-1923* (New Delhi: Philatelic Congress of India: Army Postal Service Association, 1992).

INTERNATIONAL RELATIONS

- CHINA

-- Foreign Policy: Parameters and Principles

591 Ahmed, Abu Nasar Saied. 'Mao in Shaping China's International Personality', in Girin Phukon and Dhiren

Bhagawati (Eds.), *Mao Zedong and Social Reconstruction* (New Delhi: South Asian Publishers, 1996), pp. 124-41.

592 Sinha Bhattacharjea, Mira. 'Mao: China, the World and India', in Girin Phukon and Dhiren Bhagawati (Eds.), *Mao Zedong and Social Reconstruction* (New Delhi: South Asian Publishers, 1996), pp. 103-23.

593 Tao, Wenzhao. 'Chinese Revolution and Foreign Relations', in Manoranjan Mohanty (Ed.), *Chinese Revolution: Comparative Perspectives on Transformation of Non-Western Societies* (Delhi: Ajanta Publications, 1992), pp. 115-45.

-- China-Asia, Central

594 Rahul, Ram. *Afghanistan, Mongolia and China* (New Delhi: Atlantic Publishers and Distributors, 1992).

595 Rahul, Ram. 'China, Afghanistan and Mongolia', in Ram Rahul. *China, Russia and Central Asia* (New Delhi: Vikas, 1995), pp. 70-88.

- ASIA, EAST

596 Radtke, Kurt W. 'The Pacific Area After the Collapse of the Soviet Union: Japan, China and Korea', in Kanta Ahuja, *et.al.* (Eds.), *Regime Transformations and Global Realignments: Indo-European Dialogues on the Post-Cold World War* (New Delhi: Sage Publications, 1993), pp. 227-41.

- ASIA, SOUTH

597 Ghoble, T.R. 'Some Aspects of China's Changing Outlook and South Asia', in *Indian History Congress. Proceedings of the Indian History Congress, 54th Session, 1993, Mysore* (Delhi: Indian History Congress, 1994), pp. 754-56.

598 Jain, B.M. 'The Chinese Role in South Asia', in B.M. Jain, *Nuclear Politics in South Asia: In Search of an Alternative Paradigm* (Jaipur: Rawat Publications, 1994), pp. 115-31.

599 Mojumdar, K. 'Nepal, Tibet, China and India, 1923-33: Tangled Web of Himalayan Politics', in Ramakant (Ed.), *South Asia: Some Reflections* (Jaipur: Alekh Publishers, 1993), pp. 144-68.

600 Rose, Leo E. 'Impact of Sino-Soviet-US Normalization on South Asia in the Eighties', in Shelton U. Kodikara (Ed.), *External Compulsions of South Asian Politics* (New Delhi: Sage Publications, 1993), pp. 96-106.

601 Upreti, Prem R. 'China and South Asia: A Historical Perspective', in Prem R. Upreti, *Nepal and South Asia: A Study in Continuity and Change* (New Delhi: Commonwealth Publishers, 1994), pp. 173-82.

602 Werake, Mahinda. 'China and South Asia in the Eighties', in Shelton U. Kodikara (Ed.), *External Compulsions of South Asian Politics* (New Delhi: Sage Publications, 1993), pp. 79-95.

603 Werake, Mahinda. 'The China Factor in South Asia: Myth and Realities', in D.V.J. Jayasekara (Ed.), *Security Dilemma of a Small State* (New Delhi: South Asian Publishers, 1992), Vol. 1, pp. 398-421.

-- Bangladesh

604 Ghosh, Shyamali. 'Bangladesh and China: A Stable Relationship', in S.R. Chakravarty (Ed.), *Foreign Policy of Bangladesh* (New Delhi: Har-Anand Publications, 1994), pp. 298-309.

605 Ghosh, Suchita. *China-Bangladesh-India Tangle Today: Towards a Solution?* (New Delhi: Sterling Publishers, 1995).

-- India

606 Ahuja, J.S. 'The Chinese Aggression and Indo-Pak Conflict', in J.S. Ahuja, *Second to None: A History of Punjab Police* (Ludhiana: Mohindra Bros. Printers, 1995), pp . 220-25.

607 Andersen, Walter K. 'Balancing China and the USSR', in Chandra Pal Singh (Ed.), *India in Asia* (New Delhi: Heritage Publishers, 1994), pp. 231-34.

608 Ashoka and Shubha. 'Jawaharlal Nehru: The Sinophile', in Tan Chung (Ed.), *India and China* (New Delhi: Indian Council for Cultural Relations, 1994), pp. 119-35; *Indian Horizons*, Special Issue, Vol. 43, Nos. 1-2, 1994.

609 Bajpai, Kanti P. and Coe, Bonnie L. 'Confidence Building Between India and China', in Michael Krepon and Amit

Sevak (Eds.), *Crisis Prevention; Confidence Building and Reconciliation in South Asia* (New Delhi: Manohar, 1996), pp. 199-226.

610 Bharadwaj, A.N. China Invades India', in A.N. Bharadwaj, *Failures of the UNO* (Jammu: Jay Kay Publications, 1996), pp. 135-53.

611 Bhatt, S.C. 'India-China', in S.C. Bhatt, *The Triangle, India-Nepal-China: A Study of Treaty Relations* (New Delhi: Gyan Publishing House, 1996), pp. 161-231.

612 Bhattacharjee, Ajit. 'Can the Country Afford a Repeat of 1962? in Anand Kumar (Ed.), *Tibet: A Sourcebook* (New Delhi: Radiant Publishers, 1995), pp. 23-26.

613 Bhave, Y.G. 'Nehru and Tibet and China', in Y.G. Bhave, *The First Prime Minister of India* (New Delhi: Northern Book Centre, 1995), pp. 23-29.

614 Bhave, Y.G. 'The Tibetan Folly", in Y.G. Bhave, *The First Prime Minister of India* (New Delhi: Northern Book Centre, 1995), pp. 92-95.

615 Chajuniva, Emeka. 'The Sino-Indian Border Conflict of 1962', in Emeka Chajuniva (Ed.), *India-US Security Relations, 1947-1990* (Delhi: Chanakya Publications, 1992), pp. 54-63.

616 Chandy, K.K. 'Delhi to Peking Peace March', in K.K. Chandy, *Peace Culture Amidst Power Conflicts: Caste, Class, Race, State Tensions* (Kottayam: Fellowship of Reconciliation, 1992), pp. 247-55.

617 Chandy, K.K. 'Sino-Indian Border Tension (An Appeal for Reconciliation, Arunodayam, August 1962), in K.K. Chandy, *Peace Culture Amidst Power Conflicts: Caste, Class, Race, State Tensions* (Kottayam: Fellowship of Reconciliation, 1992), pp. 309-12.

618 Chandy, K.K. 'Sino-Indian Rapprochement', in K.K. Chandy, *Peace Culture Amidst Power Conflicts: Caste, Class, Race, State Tensions* (Kottayam: Fellowship of Reconciliation, 1992), pp. 387-90.

619 Chavan, Y.B. NEFA Inquiry and Defence Preparedness (Section 2)', in *Y.B. Chavan: Selected Speeches in Parliament*; ed. by R.D. Pradhan (Pune: Ameya

Prakashan, 1995), Vol. I: Defence and House Minister, pp. 56-90. "Carries the results of an Internal Inquiry (Henderson-Brooks Committee) summarised in a Statement presented to the Rajya Sabha and Lok Sabha . . . along with another statement on 'Our Defence Preparedness'."

620 Chitkara, M.G. 'China's Involvement', in M.G. Chitkara, *Kashmir Imbroglio: Diagnosis and Remedy* (New Delhi: APH Publising Corporation, 1996), pp. 51-59.

621 Chitkara, M.G. 'Tibet', in M.G. Chitkara, *Kashmir Imbroglio: Diagnosis and Remedy* (New Delhi: APH Publication Corporation, 1996), pp. 61-73.

622 Choudhury, Deba Prosad. 'Across the Western Himalaya: Western Tibet', in Deba Prosad Choudhury, *Trade and Politics in the Himalayan-Karakoram Borderlands* (Mumbai: Orient Longman, 1996), pp. 18-34.

623 Choudhury, Deba Prosad. 'India's Boundaries with Western Tibet and Eastern Turkestan', in Deba Prosad Choudhury, *Trade and Politics in the Himalayan-Karakoram Borderlands* (Mumbai: Orient Longman, 1996), pp. 55-75.

624 Chowdhury, J.N. 'The McMahon Line', in J.N. Chowdhury, *Arunachal Panorama: A Study in Profile* (Itanagar: Directorate of Research, Arunachal Pradesh, 1992), pp. 7-10.

625 Damodran, A.K. 'Diary of an Old China Hand', in Tan Chung (Ed.), *India and China* (New Delhi: Indian Council for Cultural Relations, 1994), pp. 163-72; *Indian Horizons*, Special Issue, Vol. 43, Nos. 1-2, 1994.

626 Dandavate, Madhu. 'Sino-Indian Relations', in Madhu Dandavate, *As the Mind Unfolds: Issues and Personalities*; ed. by B. Vivekanandan (Delhi: Shipra Publications, 1993), pp. 190-93.

627 Darshan Singh. 'Ties with China', in Darshan Singh, *P.V. Narasimha Rao: The Charismatic Personality* (Delhi: R.S. Chawla, 1995), pp. 106-08.

628 Das, Bipinpal. 'Li Peng's Visit—An Evaluation', in Bipinpal Das, *On World Affairs* (Guwahati: Lawyers' Book Stall, 1992), pp. 305-314.

629 Das, Bipinpal. 'Sino-Indian Relations—Prospects and Possibilities', in Bipinpal Das, *On World Affairs* (Guwahati: Lawyers' Book Stall, 1992), pp. 295-304.

630 Das, C.R. 'Sino-Indian Relations and Nehru', in Sharada Rath (Ed.), *Jawaharlal Nehru: The Nation Builder and Architect of India's Foreign Policy* (Meerut: Anu Books, 1992), pp. 245-54.

631 Das, Nara Narayan. 'India and China: Quest for a Common Destiny', in S.D. Muni (Ed.), *Understanding South Asia: Essays in the Memory of Late Professor (Mrs.) Urmila Phadnis* (New Delhi: South Asian Publishers, 1994), pp. 1-9.

632 Datta, Rekha. 'The United States-Pakistan Alliance and the Sino-Indian Border War, 1962', in Rekha Datta, *Why Alliances Endure: The United States-Pakistan Alliance, 1954-1971* (New Delhi: South Asian Publishers, 1994), pp. 74-111.

633 Deshingkar, Giri. 'India-China Relations: The Nehru Years', in D.R. Sardesai (Ed.), *The Legacy of Nehru: A Centennial Assessment* (New Delhi: Promilla, 1992), pp. 322-43.

634 Dixit, J.N. The Chinese Enigma', in J.N. Dixit, *My South Block Years: Memoirs of a Foreign Secretary* (New Delhi: UBS Publishers' Distributors, 1996), pp. 229-52.

635 Dutt, Gargi and Dutt, V.P. 'India and China: The South Asian Equation', in Gargi Dutt and V.P. Dutt, *China After Mao* (New Delhi: Vikas Publishing House, 1991), pp. 354-412.

636 Dutta, V.P. 'USA, China and the Kashmir Conflict', in V.D. Chopra (Ed.), *Genesis of Regional Conflicts: Kashmir, Afghanistan, West Asia, Cambodia, Chechnya* (Delhi: Gyan Publishing House, 1995), pp. 63-71.

637 Dutta, Sujit. 'India's Evolving Relations with China', in Dipankar Banerjee (Ed.), *Towards an Era of Cooperation: An Indo-Australian Dialogue* (New Delhi: Institute for Defence Studies and Analyses, 1995), pp. 63-88.

638 Dwivedy, Surendranath. 'PSP's Finest Hour in the Lok Sabha: Role During the China-India War', in D. Sundar Ram (Ed.), *Readings in the Indian Parliamentary Opposition*

(New Delhi: Kanishka Publishers' Distributors, 1996), pp. 107-18.

639 Fernandes, George. 'Tibet, China, Asia and the World Conscience', in Anand Kumar (Ed.), *Tibet: A Sourcebook* (New Delhi: Radiant Publishers, 1995), pp. 7-15.

640 Gandhi, M.K. 'Gandhi's Letter to General Chiang Kai-shek', in D.C. Jha, *Mahatma Gandhi, the Congress and the Partition of India* (New Delhi: Sanchar Publishing House, 1995), pp. 138-43.

640A Ghoble, T.R. 'Some Aspects of Sino-Indian Relations During the Nehru Era (1959)', in Barun De, *et.al.* (Eds.), *Proceedings of the Indian History Congress, 56th Session, 1995, Rabindra Bharati University* (Calcutta: Firma KLM, 1996), pp. 833-45.

641 Gill, S.S. 'India-China Showdown', in S.S. Gill, *The Dynasty: A Political Biography of the Premier Ruling Family of Modern India* (New Delhi: Harper-Collins Publishers, India, 1996), pp. 188-200.

642 Gour, Neelam Saran. *Speaking of '62: A Novel* (New Delhi: Penguin Books India, 1995).

643 Grover, Verinder (Ed.), *China, Japan, and India's Foreign Policy* (New Delhi: Deep and Deep Publications, 1992).

644 Hazarika, Joysankar. 'The Birth of the McMahon Line', in Joysankar Hazarika, *Geopolitics of Northeast India: A Strategical Study* (New Delhi: Gyan Publishing House, 1996), pp. 124-31.

645 Hazarika, Joysankar. 'The Inner Line, the Outer Line and the Birth of McMahon Line and Associated Problems', in Joysankar Hazarika, *Geopolitics of Northeast India: A Strategical Study* (New Delhi: Gyan Publishing House, 1996), pp. 121-36.

646 Hazarika, Joysankar. 'North-East Frontier of India and China's Claim', in Joysankar Hazarika, *Geopolitics of Northeast India: A Strategical Study* (New Delhi: Gyan Publishing House, 1996), pp. 131-40.

647 Hsueh. 'Speech by Hsueh (China) in Security Council, 1241st Meeting, September 18, 1965', in J.C. Aggarwal

and S.P. Aggarwal, *Modern History of Jammu and Kashmir* (Delhi: Concept Publishing Company, 1995), pp. 426-28.

648 'Huan Xin Chuan', in *My India, The India Eternal* by Swami Vivekananda (Calcutta: Ramakrishna Mission Institute of Culture, 1993), pp. 243-45; "From a speech delivered by Huan Xin Chuan on 'Vivekananda and China', at the Asiatic Society, Calcutta, on 4 January 1980.

649 Hussain, T. Karki. 'India, China and Southeast Asia After the Cold War', in Baladas Ghoslal (Ed.), *India and Southeast Asia: Challenges and Opportunities* (Delhi: Konark Publishers, 1996), pp. 41-53.

650 Hussain, T. Karki. 'India-China Detente Destined to Succeed', in Tan Chung (Ed.), *China and India* (New Delhi: Indian Council for Cultural Relations, 1994), pp. 317-27; *Indian Horizons*, Special Issue, Vol. 43, Nos. 1-2, 1994.

651 Hussain, T. Karki. 'India-China Relations: Towards the Year 2000 A.D.', in R.S. Yadav (Ed.), *India's Foreign Policy Towards 2000 A.D.* (New Delhi: Deep and Deep Publications, 1993), pp. 93-102.

652 Imam, Zafar. 'India-China Relations in Soviet Perspective', in Zafar Imam. *New Russia: Disintegration and Crisis: Contemporary Chronicle, 1988-1994* (New Delhi: ABC Publishing House, 1995), pp. 13-17.

653 India and People's Republic of China. 'Agreements Between China and India', in Michael Krepon and Amit Sevak (Eds.), *Crisis Prevention, Confidence Building and Reconciliation in South Asia* (New Delhi: Manohar, 1996), pp. 261-70.

Includes the texts of "Agreement on Trade and Intercourse Between Tibet Region of China and India, April 29, 1954 (Peking)"; "Agreement on the Maintenance of Peace and Tranquility Along the Line of Actual Control in the India-China Border Areas, September 7, 1993 (Beijing)"; "Agreement on Environmental Cooperation", September 7, 1993 (Beijing); etc.

654 Jain, C.K. 'India-China Border Dispute, Chinese Aggression, India-China Relations', in C.K. Jain (Ed.), *Lal Bahadur Shastri and Parliament* (New Delhi: Lok Sabha Secretariat, 1993), pp. 508-9; 518-9; 593-644.

655 Jasjit Singh (Ed.), *India, China and Panchsheel* (New Delhi: Sanchar Publishing House, 1996).

656 Joginder Singh. 'Sino-Indian Border Conflict 1962', in Joginder Singh, *Behind the Scene: An Analysis of India's Military Operations, 1947-1971* (New Delhi: Lancer International, 1993), pp. 39-46.

657 Joshi, Manoj. 'India, China and the Asian Century', in Tan Chung (Ed.), *China and India* (New Delhi: Indian Council for Cultural Relations, 1994), pp. 343-52; *Indian Horizons*, Special Issue, Vol. 43, Nos. 1-2, 1994.

658 Kashyap, Subhash C. 'China Aggression', in Subhash C. Kashyap, *History of the Parliament of India* (Delhi: Shipra Publication, 1996), Vol. 3, pp. 16-21.

659 Kaushik, S.L. 'Political and Economic Aspects of Sino-Indian Relations', in S.L. Kaushik (Ed.), *Modern Governments and Political Systems* (New Delhi: Mittal Publications, 1995), pp. 196-269.

660 Kewal Singh. 'The India-China Border War of 1962', in Kewal Singh, *Partition and Aftermath: Memoirs of an Ambassador* (New Delhi: Vikas, 1991), pp. 124-48.

661 Khanna, Manuka. 'China', in Manuka Khanna, *Indo-US Relations During the Presidency of Ronald Reagan* (New Delhi: Classical Publishing Company, 1996), pp. 150-59.

662 Khilnani, N.M. 'China and India', in N.M. Khilnani, *New Dimensions of Indian Foreign Policy: Prime Minister Narasimha Rao's Era X-rayed* (New Delhi: Westwill Publishing House, 1995), pp. 165-69.

663 Kler, Gurdip Singh. *Unsung Battles of 1962* (New Delhi: Lancer Publishers, 1995).

664 Kohli, Manorama. 'Loss of Tibet and Impact on Indo-Bhutan Relations', in Manorama Kohli, *From Dependency to Interdependence: A Study of Indo-Bhutan Relations* (New Delhi: Vikas Publishing House, 1993), pp. 54-79.

665 Kohli, Manorama. 'Sino-Indian Conflict and Domestic Developments in Bhutan (1962-71)', in Manorama Kohli, *From Dependency to Interdependence: A Study of Indo-Bhutan Relations* (New Delhi: Vikas Publishing House, 1993), pp. 80-92.

666 Longer, V. 'Fighting on India-China Border', in V. Longer, *Our Bravest Warriors* (New Delhi: Publications Division, Ministry of Information and Broadcasting, Government of India, 1990), pp. 15-22.

667 Ludra, Kuldip S. 'India and China', in Kuldip Ludra, *Understanding War, Its Implications and Effects* (Chandigarh: Kuldip S. Ludra, 1992), pp. 77-85.

668 Majumdar, Charu. 'Develop Revolutionary War to Eliminate War of Aggression Against China', in Suniti Kumar Ghosh (Ed.), *The Historic Turning Point: A Liberation Anthology* (Calcutta: S.K. Gosh, 1993), Vol. 2, pp. 42-45; *From Liberation*, Vol. 2, 12 October 1969.

669 Malviya, Gopalji. *Sino-Indian Relations: Security Environment in Nineties* (Madras: University of Madras, 1992).

670 Mathur, Krishan D. 'Foreign Policy of P.V. Narasimha Rao: China and Revival of Panchsheel Spirit', in Krishan D. Mathur, *Conduct of India's Foreign Policy* (New Delhi: South Asian Publishers, 1996), pp. 158-61.

671 Mehra, Parshotam. *An 'Agreed Frontier': Ladakh and India's Northernmost Borders, 1846-1947* (Delhi: Oxford University Press, 1993).

672 Mehta, Jagat S. 'India-China Relations: A Review and Prognosis', in V.A. Pai Panandiker (Ed.), *India's Policy Problems* (Delhi: Konark Publishers, 1996), Vol. 2, pp. 216-45.

673 Menon, K.P.S. 'Interwoven Memories', in Tan Chung (Ed.), *China and India* (New Delhi: Indian Council for Cultural Relations, 1994), pp. 141-48; *Indian Horizons*, Special Issue, Vol. 43, Nos. 1-2, 1994.

674 Mishra, Rajan Kumar. 'India and China: Cautious Optimism', in Ranjan Kumar Mishra, *India and International Relations* (New Delhi: Kanishka Publishers Distributors, 1996), pp. 161-76.

675 Mishra, S.N. 'India and East Asia', in S.N. Mishra, *India: The Cold War Years* (New Delhi: South Asian Publishers, 1994), pp. 139-57.

676 Mohanty, Jitendra Nath. 'Soviet Factor in Sino-Indian Relations: Nehru Era', in Sharada Nath (Ed.), *Jawaharlal Nehru: The Nation Builder and Architect of India's Foreign Policy* (Meerut: Anu Books, 1992), pp. 255-62.

677 Naik, J.A. 'China in Russia's Relations with India', in J.A. Naik, *Russian Policy Towards India: From Stalin to Yeltsin* (New Delhi: M.D. Publications, 1995), pp. 131-48.

678 Namboodiripad, E.M.S. 'Border Conflict with China', in E.M.S. Namboodiripad, *The Communist Party in Kerala: Six Decades of Struggle and Advance* (New Delhi: National Book Centre, 1994), pp. 201-05.

679 Natarajan, V.C. '1962 Debacle', in V.C. Natarajan, *Defence Reporting in India: The Communication Gap* (Noida: Trishul Publications, 1994), pp. 42-45.

680 Nehru, Jawaharlal. 'India and China', in Tan Chung (Ed.), *China and India* (New Delhi: Indian Council for Cultural Relations, 1994), pp. 115-18; *Indian Horizons*, Special Issue, Vol. 43, Nos. 1-2, 1994. "Presidential Address at the Fifth Annual General Meeting of the Sino-Indian Cultural Society held at Santiniketan on December 28, 1945. Also, in *The Sino-Indian Journal*, Vol. 1, Pt. 1, July 1947".

681 Paranjpe, V.V. 'India and China: Some Memories, Some Reflections', in Tan Chung (Ed.), *China and India* (New Delhi: Indian Council for Cultural Relations, 1994), pp. 149-62; *Indian Horizons*, Special Issue, Vol. 43, Nos. 1-2, 1994.

682 Patil, Shivraj V. 'China', in Shivraj V. Patil, *Emerging Vision of India* (Ladnun, Rajasthan: Jain Vishva Bharati; New Delhi: Distributed by D.K. Publishers Distributors, 1996), pp. 125-26.

683 Paulose, Thomas. 'India and China: The Asian Context', in Thomas Paulose and Gurpeet Kaur (Eds.), *India and World Affairs* (New Delhi: Anmol Publications, 1996), pp. 165-78.

684 Rajan, M.S. 'Chinese Aggression and the Future of India's Non-Alignment Policy', in M.S. Rajan, *Studies in India's Foreign Policy* (New Delhi: ABC Publishing House, 1993), pp. 290-307.

685 Ramachandran, Sita. 'Regional Environment-I: Sino-Indian Relations and Sino-Pak Relations', in Sita Ramachandran, *Decision-Making in Foreign Policy* (New Delhi: Northern Book Centre, 1996), pp. 86-122.

686 Reddy, Ram Gopal. 'Letter to Prime Minister P.V. Narasimha Rao on His Successful Visit of China and Korea', in Ram Gopal Reddy, *Life and Letters of Ram Gopal Reddy: Legislator and Parliamentarian*, edited by N.K. Acharya (Hyderabad: M.V. Srinivasa Reddy, 1995), p. 42.

687 Roy, Meenu. 'The Chinese War and the United States', in Meenu Roy. *Thousand Days of Indo-US Diplomacy: The Kennedy-Nehru Era* (New Delhi: Deep and Deep Publications, 1993), pp. 79-122.

688 Sharma, Satish Kumar. 'India-China Relations in 1990s: An Analysis of External Environment', in R.S. Yadav (Ed.), *India's Foreign Policy Towards 2000 A.D.* (New Delhi: Deep and Deep Publications, 1993), pp. 103-10.

689 Singh, L.P. 'The Chinese Aggression', in L.P. Singh, *Portrait of Lal Bahadur Shastri: A Quintessential Gandhian* (Delhi: Ravi Dayal, 1996), pp. 50-66.

690 H.S. Sondhi. 'The Indo-Chinese War—1962', in H.S. Sondhi, *Top Brass: A Critical Appraisal of the Indian Military Leadership* (Noida: Trishul Publications, 1993), pp. 21-46.

691 Srivastava, C.P. 'The Chinese Ultimatum', in C.P. Srivastava, *Lal Bahadur Shastri, Prime Minister of India, 4 June 1964 - 11 January 1966: A Life of Truth in Politics* (Delhi: Oxford University Press, 1995), pp. 273-91.

692 Subramaniam, C. 'Chinese Aggression', in C. Subramaniam, *Hand of Destiny: Memoirs* (Bombay: Bharatiya Vidya Bhavan, 1995), Vol. 2, pp. 44-54.

693 Surkhang, Kalen and Peshi, Dapon. 'Tibetan Letter of Agreement, 1842', and 'Agreement Between Tibet and Kashmir (1852)', in Jaswant Singh, *Jammu and Kashmir:*

Political and Constitutional Development (New Delhi: Har-Anand Publications, 1996), pp. 44-45.

694 Tagore, Rabindranath, 'China and India', in Rabindranath Tagore, *The English Writings of Rabindranath Tagore;* ed. by Sisir Kumar Das (New Delhi: Sahitya Akademi, 1996), Vol. 3: A Miscellany, pp. 711-15.

695 Tan, Chung. 'Dawn of India-China Detente', in Satish Kumar (Ed.), *Yearbook on India's Foreign Policy 1990-91* (New Delhi: Tata McGraw-Hill Publishing Company, 1991), pp. 47-64.

696 Telang, G.M. 'The Kashmir Question—Hint of Chinese Interest in Promoting a Solution', in Gull Mohd. (Comp.), *Kashmir: From Autonomy to Azadi* (Srinagar: Valley Book House, 1996), pp. 219-22.

697 Tewari, K.K. 'Chinese Attack on India—October 1962', in K.K. Tewari, *A Soldier's Voyage of Self-Discovery* (Pondicherry: Sri Aurobindo Memorial Fund Society, 1995), pp. 58-77.

698 Tewari, K.K. 'Reflections on the India-China War of 1962', in K.K. Tewari, *A Soldier's Voyage of Self-Discovery* (Pondicherry: Sri Aurobindo Memorial Fund Society, 1995), pp. 112-24.

699 Thomas, Mathew. 'The Watershed: Sino-Indian Conflict 1962', in Mathew Thomas, *Lt. Gen. P.S. Bhagat, PVSM, VC: A Biography* (New Delhi: Lancer International, 1994), pp. 221-45.

700 Tyagi, Narendra Kumar. 'India's Relations with the People's Republic of China', in Narendra Kumar Tyagi, *Rediscovering India* (Bombay: Bharatiya Vidya Bhavan, 1995), pp. 281-93.

701 Vajpayee, Atal Bihari. 'China', in Atal Bihari Vajpayee, *Four Decades in Parliament;* edited by N.M. Ghatate (Delhi: Shipra Publications, 1996), Vol. 3, *Foreign Affairs*, pp. 170-216.

702 Vajpayee, Atal Bihari. 'Visit to China', in Atal Bihari Vajpayee, *Four Decades in Parliament;* edited by N.M. Ghatate (Delhi: Shipra Publications, 1996), Vol. 3, *Foreign Affairs*, pp. 209-14.

703 Vasudevan, Parvathi. 'The Challenge: The Impact of Chinese Aggression', in Parvathi Vasudevan, *Non-Alignment as a Factor in Indo-American Relations: The Nehru Era* (Delhi: Kalinga Publications, 1996), pp. 127-51.

704 Yohra, Sahdev. *The Northern Frontier of India: The Border Dispute with China* (New Delhi: Intellectual Publishing House, 1993).

705 Wang, Hongju. 'Sino-Indian Relations—Past and Future', in Jasjit Singh (Ed.), *India, China and Panchsheel* (New Delhi: Sanchar Publishing House, 1996), pp. 144-59.

706 Yadav, Lal Babu. *Indo-Bhutan Relations and China Interventions* (New Delhi: Anmol Publications, 1996).

707 Yasin, Madhavi. 'Anglo-Tibetan Relations', in Madhavi Yasin, *India's Foreign Policy: The Dufferin Years* (New Delhi: Raj Publications, 1994), pp. 176-211.

708 Zhao, Weiwen and Deshingkar, Giri. 'Improving Sino-Indo Relations', in Michael Krepon and Amit Sevak (Eds.), *Crisis Prevention, Confidence Building and Reconciliation in South Asia* (New Delhi: Manohar, 1996), pp. 227-38.

- CONSULAR OFFICES

-- Directories

709 'China', in India, Ministry of External Affairs, *Consular Offices in India, September 1995* (New Delhi: Protocol Division, Ministry of External Affairs, Government of vIndia, 1995), pp. 6-7.

-- Treaties and Agreements

710 India and China. 'Sino-Indian Agreement (7 September 1993)', in J.N. Dixit, *My South Block Years: Memoirs of a Foreign Secretary* (New Delhi: UBS Publishers' Distributors, 1996), pp. 460-63.

-- Nepal

711 Bhasin, Avtar Singh (Ed.), *Nepal's Relations with India and China: Documents, 1947-1992* (Delhi: Siba Exim, 1994).

712 Bhatt, S.C. 'Nepal-China', in S.C. Bhatt, *The Triangle, India-Nepal-China: A Study of Treaty Relations* (New Delhi: Gyan Publishing House, 1996), pp. 109-160.

713 Dharamdasani, M.D. China as a Factor', in Ramakant, *Indo-Nepal Relations* (New Delhi: South Asian Publishers, 1992), pp. 293-300.

714 Ghildial, Nalineet. 'Indo-Nepal Relations and China', in Ramakant, *Indo-Nepal Relations* (New Delhi: South Asian Publishers, 1992), pp. 316-30.

715 Ghoble, T.R. 'India and China-Nepal Relations 1950-80: An Appraisal', in *Proceedings of the Indian History Congress, 53rd Session (1992-93), Warangal, 1993* (Delhi: Indian History Congress, 1993), pp. 598-606.

716 Laksman Bahadur, K.C. 'Nepal, India and China Relations', in K.C. Laksman Bahadur, *Recent Nepal: An Analysis of Recent Democratic Upsurge and Its Aftermath* (Jaipur: Nirala Publications, 1993), pp. 145-49.

717 Mahapatra, Chintamani. 'Nepal in China's South Asian Strategy', in M.D. Dharmadasani (Ed.), *Democratic Nepal* (Varanasi: Shalimar Publishing House, 1992), pp. 123-43.

718 Sever, Adrian. 'Complementary Missions to China', in Adrian Sever, *Aspects of Modern Nepalese History* (New Delhi: Vikas Publishing House, 1996), pp. 167-70.

719 Sever, Adrian. 'Relations with Tibet', in Adrian Sever, *Aspects of Modern Nepalese History* (New Delhi: Vikas Publishing House, 1996), pp. 171-84.

720 Singh, Shiva Bahadur. 'The China Factor', in Shiva Bahadur Singh, *Indo-Nepalese Relations: Discord and Harmony* (Varanasi: Ganga Kaveri Publishing House, 1994), pp. 110-32.

721 Suwal, Yashoda. 'Sino-Indian Relations and Nepal', in Ramakant, *Indo-Nepal Relations* (New Delhi: South Asian Publishers, 1992), pp. 301-15.

-- Pakistan

722 Chitkara, M.G. 'Nuclear China', in M.G. Chitkara, *Nuclear Pakistan* (New Delhi: APH Publishing Corporation, 1996), p. 163-92.

723 Grover, Verinder and Arora, Ranjana (Eds.). 'Pakistan's Relations with China, Russia and Muslim Soviets', in Verinder Grover and Ranjana Arora (Eds.), *Political System in Pakistan* (New Delhi: Deep and Deep Publications, 1995), Vol. 9.

724 Naqvi, Saeed. 'Geneva Outcome, Iranian Puzzle and China', in Saeed Naqvi, *The Last Brahmin Prime Minister?* (New Delhi: Har-Anand Publications, 1996), pp. 128-31.

725 Saha, B.P. 'Sino-Pakistan Relations', in B.P. Saha, *Trans-Border Terrorism: Internationalisation of Kashmir Tangle* (New Delhi: Har-Anand Publications, 1996), pp. 256-8.

- ASIA, WEST

726 Chanukya, D. 'Chinese Role', in D. Chanukya, *The Political History of Middle East Crisis, August 1990-February 1991: Big Fives' Role in Operation Desert Shield and Operation Desert Storm* (Hyderabad: Megha Hills, 1992), pp. 123-28 .

727 Choedon, Yeshi. 'China: Domestic Constrains', in A.K. Pasha, *The Gulf in Turmoil: A Global Response* (New Delhi: Lancers Books, 1992), pp. 266-75.

- ASIA, SOUTHEAST

-- Burma

728 Pakem, P. 'China and the Shifts in Indo-Burmese Relations', in P. Pakem, *India-Burma Relations* (New Delhi: Omsons Publications, 1992), pp. 182-200.

729 Pakem, P. 'The Sino-Burmese Border and its Effects on the Indo-Burmese Relations', in P. Pakem, *India-Burma Relations* (New Delhi: Omsons Publications, 1992), pp. 84-102.

-- Thailand

730 Tsui, Chak Wing David. *China and the Communist Armed Struggle in Thailand* (New Delhi: Radiant Publishers, 1995).

-- Vietnam

731 Vajpayee, Atal Bihari. 'Chinese Invasion of Vietnam', in Atal Bihari Vajpayee, *Four Decades in Parliament*, edited

by N.M. Ghatate (Delhi: Shipra Publications, 1996), *Foreign Affairs*, Vol. 3, pp. 381-84.

- EUROPE

-- Soviet Russia

732 Brar, Bhupinder. 'The Sino-Soviet Split', in Bhupinder Brar, *Explaining Communist Crisis* (Delhi: Ajanta Publications, 1994), pp. 23-93.

733 Rahul, Ram. *China, Russia and Central Asia* (New Delhi: Vikas, 1995).

- USA

734 Madan, Vijay. 'The Likely United States Policy in South Asia and its Impact on India, Pakistan and China', in Vijay Madan, *Indo-Pak Relations: Viewpoints, 1989-1996* (New Delhi: Lancer Publishers, 1996), pp. 144-55.

735 Raghavan, Sudha. 'Southeast Asian Countries and Their Attitudes Towards the Indian Ocean Power Politics', in Sudha Raghavan, *The Indian Ocean Power Politics: Attitudes of South East Asian and South Pacific Countries* (New Delhi: Lancers Books, 1996), pp. 187-382.

736 Ramachandran, Sita. 'Global Environment: Triangular Relations, Sino-American Relations and Sino-Soviet Relations', in Sita Ramachandran, *Decision-Making in Foreign Policy* (New Delhi: Northern Book Centre, 1996), pp. 62-85.

- INDIAN OCEAN

737 Yadav, R.S. 'Soviet-Chinese Rift and Indian Ocean States', in R.S. Yadav, *From Ideology to Pragmatism: A Study of Soviet and Russian Policy Towards the Indian Ocean* (Kurukshetra: National Book Agency, 1995), pp. 48-65.

- PACIFIC COUNTRIES

738 Kent, Ann. 'Australian-China Relations: The Long View, 1965-1995', in Dipankar Banerjee (Ed.), *Towards An Era of Cooperation: An Indo-Australian Dialogue* (New Delhi: Institute for Defence Studies and Analyses, 1995), pp. 89-136.

- UNITED NATIONS

739 Bharadwaj, A.N. 'Chinese Efforts for UN Berth', in A.N. Bharadwaj, *Failures of the UNO* (Jammu: Jay Kay Publications, 1996), pp. 83-85.

740 Sud, Usha. 'Question of China's Membership, and India Supports Chinese Representation', in Usha Sud, *United Nations and India: Saga of Cooperation* (New Delhi: Vikas Publishing House, 1996), pp. 65-68.

- WORLD

741 Das, Naranarayan. 'China and the Changing World Order', in Alokesh Barua, *Global Order: Recent Changes and Responses* (New Delhi: Lancers Books, 1992), pp. 140-55.

742 Rahul, Ram. 'China's Other Boundaries', in Ram Rahul, *Central Asia: Major Perspectives* (New Delhi: Vikas, 1993), pp. 40-58.

- EAST ASIA-UN

743 Chakraborty, Bimal. 'Intervention in Third World Affairs', in Bimal Chakraborty, *The United Nations and the Third World: Shifting Paradigms* (New Delhi: Tata McGraw-Hill Publishing Company, 1996), pp. 60-62.

- JAPAN

-- Foreign Policy: Parameters And Principles

744 Ghosh, B.N. and Tanahashi, T.K. 'Japan's Chequebook Diplomay', in B.N. Ghosh, *Economic Development and Social Change: Some Contemporary Problems* (New Delhi: Deep and Deep Publications, 1996), pp. 110-15.

- ASIA, EAST

-- China

745 Limaya, Madhu. 'Pacific Quadrangle: US-Japan-China-Russia Relations', in Madhu Limaye, *Last Writings* (Delhi: B.R. Publishing Corporation, 1996), pp. 98-102.

746 Verma, Lalima. *Making of Japan's China Policy* (Delhi: Kalinga Publications, 1991).

- ASIA SOUTH

747 Abe, Shigeyuki. 'South Asia and Japan: Prospects for Further Cooperation', in S.P. Gupta, *et.al.* (Eds.), *South Asia as a Dynamic Partner: Papers Presented at the Conference on South Asia as a Dynamic Partner; Prospects for the Future*, held at New Delhi, May 25-27 1992 (New Delhi: Macmillan, 1994), pp. 243-89.

748 Hirose, Takako. 'Japan in a Dilemma: The Search for a Horizontal Japan-South Asia Relationship', in Purnendra Jain, *Distant Asian Neighbours: Japan and South Asia* (New Delhi: Sterling Publishers, 1996), pp. 28-47.

749 Hussain, Syed Noor. *Japan Not in the West: A South Asian Perception of Japan Today* (New Delhi: Vikas, 1994).

750 Jain, Purnendra C. (Eds.). *Distant Asian Neighbours: Japan and South Asia* (New Delhi: Sterling Publishers, 1996); "Papers Presented at the Workshop on Japan and South Asia, held at Oxford in June 1993."

751 Jain, Purnendra C. 'Japan and South Asia: An Overview', in Purnendra Jain, *Distant Asian Neighbours: Japan and South Asia* (New Delhi: Sterling Publishers, 1996), pp. 1-27.

752 Jain, Purnendra C. 'Japan and South Asia: Where To From Here', in Purnendra Jain, *Distant Asian Neighbours: Japan and South Asia* (New Delhi: Sterling Publishers, 1996), pp. 195-223.

753 Kesavan, K.V. 'Foreign Policies of South Asian Nations: Does Japan Matter?', in Purnendra Jain, *Distant Asian Neighbours: Japan and South Asia* (New Delhi: Sterling Publishers, 1996), pp. 48-63.

754 Panda, Rajaram. 'Japan and South Asia: Focus on India', in Rajaram Panda, *Japan and the Third World: Political and Economic Relations, 1980s-1990s* (New Delhi: Lancers Books, 1994), pp. 79-177.

755 Verma, Lalima. 'Japan and South Asia: Its Relations with Bangladesh', in S.R. Chakravarty (Ed.), *Foreign Policy of Bangladesh* (New Delhi: Har-Anand Publications, 1994), pp. 310-15.

-- Bangladesh

756 Abul Kalam. 'Bangladesh and Japan: Linkages and Developing Relationships', in Purnendra Jain, *Distant Asian Neighbours: Japan and South Asia* (New Delhi: Sterling Publishers, 1996), pp. 108-36.

-- India

757 Dixit, J.N. 'Japan: An Emerging Power', in J.N. Dixit, *My South Block Years: Memoirs of a Foreign Secretary* (New Delhi: UBS Publishers' Distributors, 1996), pp. 253-65.

758 Dutt, N.V.B.S. *Yayoi People and Ancient Indo-Japanese Relations* (New Delhi: Northern Book Centre, 1993).

759 Khilnani, N.M. 'Narasimha Rao Charms Germans and Enchants the Japanese', in N.M. Khilnani, *New Dimensions of Indian Foreign Policy: Prime Minister Narasimha Rao's Era X-rayed* (New Delhi: Westwill Publishing House, 1995) pp. 176-79.

760 Nara, Tsuyoshi. 'Swami Vivekananda and the Japanese', in *Swami Vivekananda: A Hundred Years Since Chicago, A Commemorative Volume* (Balur: Ramakrishna Math and Ramakrishna Mission, 1994), pp. 870-74.

761 Patil, Shivraj V. 'Japan', in Shivraj V. Patil, *Emerging Vision of India* (Ladnun, Rajasthan: Jain Vishva Bharati; New Delhi: Distributed by D.K. Publishers Distributors, 1996), pp. 133-34.

762 Sareen, Tilak. *Indian Revolutionaries, Japan and British Imperialism* (New Delhi: Anmol Publications, 1993), pp. 1-55.

763 Shaikh, Adam Usman. 'Our Japanese Sojourn', in Adam Usman Shaikh, *Vignettes of My Civil Service Life* (Bombay: Shad Adam Shaikh Trust, 1991), pp. 217-28.

764 Tyabji, Badr-ud-din. 'Japan (1964-1967)', in Badr-ud-din Tyabji, *Memoirs of an Egoist* (New Delhi: Roli Books, 1994), pp. 193-278.

- CONSULAR OFFICES

-- Directories

765 'Japan' in India, Ministry of External Affairs, *Consular Offices in India, September 1995* (New Delhi: Protocol

Division, Ministry of External Affairs, Government of India, 1995), pp. 25-27.

- TREATIES AND AGREEMENTS

766 'Agreement Between the Government of India and the Government of Japan for the Establishment of a Training Centre for Marine Products Processing, New Delhi, 31 March 1962', in *India: Bilateral Treaties and Agreements* (Delhi: Policy Planning and Research Division, Ministry of External Affairs, Government of India, New Delhi, by Siba Exim, 1994), Vol. 4 (1964-66), pp. 171-75.

767 'Agreement Between the Government of India and the Government of Japan for the Establishment of Agricultural Demonstration Farms, New Delhi, 23 April 1962', in *India: Bilateral Treaties and Agreements* (Delhi: Policy Planning and Research Division, Ministry of External Affairs, Government of India, New Delhi, by Siba Exim, 1994), Vol. 4 (1964-66), pp. 179-82.

768 'Agreement Between the Government of India and the Government of Japan Regarding Settlement of Certain Indian Claims, Tokyo, 14 December 1963', in *India: Bilateral Treaties and Agreements* (Delhi: Policy Planning and Research Division, Ministry of External Affairs, Government of India, New Delhi by Siba Exim, 1994), Vol. 4 (1964-66), pp. 491-94.

769 'Agreement on the Exchange of International Money Orders Between the Government of India and the Government of Japan, New Delhi, 24 February 1965', in *India: Bilateral Treaties and Agreements* (Delhi: Policy Planning and Research Division, Ministry of External Affairs, Government of India, New Delhi, by Siba Exim, 1994), Vol. 5 (1964-66), pp. 237-44.

770 'Protocol Modifying and Supplementing the Agreement Between the Government of India and the Government of Japan for the Avoidance of Double Taxation in Respect of Taxes on Income, New Delhi, 8 April 1969', in *India: Bilateral Treaties and Agreements* (Delhi: Policy Planning and Research Division, Ministry of External Affairs, Government of India, New Delhi, by Siba Exim, 1994), Vol. 6 (1964-66), pp. 382-92.

-- Nepal

771 Baral, Ishwar. 'The Status of and Future Prospects for Cultural Exchanges and Cooperation Between Nepal and Japan', in K.S. Mathew (Ed.), *Mariners, Merchants and Oceans: Studies in Maritime History* (New Delhi: Manohar Publishers and Distributors, 1995), pp. 75-77.

772 Gyawali, Dipak. 'Nepal-Japan Relations: Traditional Ties and Modern Development Aid', in Purnendra Jain, *Distant Asian Neighbours: Japan and South Asia* (New Delhi: Sterling Publishers, 1996), pp. 175-94.

-- Pakistan

773 Malik, Iftikhar H. 'Pakistan-Japan Relations: A Study in Asian Bilateralism', in Purnendra Jain, *Distant Asian Neighbours: Japan and South Asia* (New Delhi: Sterling Publishers, 1996), pp. 137-61.

774 Wijayasiri, G. 'Sri Lanka-Japan Relations', in Purnendra Jain, *Distant Asian Neighbours: Japan and South Asia* (New Delhi: Sterling Publishers, 1996), pp. 162-74.

- ASIA, SOUTHEAST

775 Panda, Rajaram. 'Japan and Southeast Asia', in Rajaram Panda, *Japan and the Third World: Political and Economic Relations, 1980s-1990s* (New Delhi: Lancers Books, 1994), pp. 19-77.

- ASIA, SOUTHEAST

776 Nagesh, Narayana. 'Japan-Philippines Political Relations During Marco's Era', in Narayana Nagesh, *Japan's Economic Diplomacy in Southeast Asia* (New Delhi: Lancers Books, 1996), pp. 35-54.

777 Panda, Rajaram. 'Japan and Southwest Asia', in Rajaram Panda, *Japan and the Third World: Political and Economic Relations, 1980s-1990s* (New Delhi: Lancers Books, 1994), pp. 179-248.

- ASIA, WEST

778 Prabhakar, H.S. 'Japan: Restrained Influence', in A.K. Pasha, *The Gulf in Turmoil: A Global Response* (New Delhi: Lancers Books, 1992), pp. 238-65.

- WORLD

779 Chakrabarty, S.K. 'Nippon—The Rising Sun in the New World Perspective', in S.K. Chakrabarty, *Aspects of Modern International Relations* (New Delhi: Mittal Publications, 1995), pp. 198-237.

780 Kesavan, K.V. 'Japan's Foreign Policy in the Changing Post-Cold War Scenario', in Shams-ud-din (Ed.), *Perspectives on the Emerging World Order* (New Delhi: Gyan Publishing House, 1995), pp. 82-90.

781 Mishra, Ranjan Kumar. 'Japan: Land of the Rising Yen', in Ranjan Kumar Mishra (Ed.), *International Relations and Political Alliances* (New Delhi: Kanishka Publishers Distributors, 1996), pp. 199-216.

782 Prabhakar, H.S. 'Japan's Expanding Role', in Sushil Kumar (Ed.), *Gorbachev's Reforms and International Change* (New Delhi: Lancers Books, 1993), pp. 154-65.

-- World, Third

783 Panda, Rajaram. *Japan and the Third World: Political and Economic Relations, 1980s-1990s* (New Delhi: Lancers Books, 1994).

- TAIWAN (ROC)

-- India

784 Dixit, J.N. 'South Africa, Israel and Taiwan: New Beginnings', in J.N. Dixit, *My South Block Years: Memoirs of a Foreign Secretary* (New Delhi: UBS Publishers' Distributors, 1996), pp. 304-16.

LANGUAGES

CHINESE

- GRAMMAR AND LEXICON

785 Nagarajan, Hemalatha. 'Xiamen Tone Sandhi', in Hemalatha Nagarajan, *A Theory of Post-Syntactic Phonology* (Madras: T.R. Publications, 1994), pp. 128-33.

786 Pattanayak, D.P. 'Languages for the Masses and Chinese Language in India', in D.P. Pattanayak, *Language,*

Education and Culture (Mysore: Central Institute of Indian Languages, 1991), pp. 61-69.

787 Zograph, I.T. 'Grammar and Lexicon in Chinese: A Dynamic Approach', in Ashin Dasgupta (Ed.), *M.M. Vidhusekhar Sastri Commemoration Volume* (Santiniketan: Research Publications, Visva Bharati, 1990), Vol. 1, pp. 83-91 (Visva-Bharati Annals, New Series; 2-3).

- SCRIPT STRUCTURE

788 Subbarayappa, B.V. 'Chinese Numerals and Chinese Numbers', in B.V. Subbarayappa, *Indus Script, Its Nature and Structure* (Madras: New Era Publications, 1996), pp. 30-31.

- STUDY AND TEACHING

789 Rawat, D.S. 'Notes on Chinese Language Teaching', in Y.C. Bhatnagar, *Foreign Language Teaching (FLT) in India* (Delhi: Ajanta Publications, 1994), pp. 179-84.

790 Tan, Chung. 'Binary Transmission in Second Language Teaching', in Y.C. Bhatnagar, *Foreign Language Teaching (FLT) in India* (Delhi: Ajanta Publications, 1994), pp. 172-78.

791 Ray, H.P. 'Problems of Translation From Chinese into Hindi', in G. Gopinathan and S. Kandaswamy (Eds.), Problems of Translation: An International Symposium Through Correspondence on the Linguistic Problems of Translation Between Hindi and Other Major Languages of the World (Allahabad: Lokbharti Prakashan, 1993), pp. 143-49.

- TRANSLATION

792 Dikshit, G.S. 'Excellence of Chinese Translations of Sanskrit Classics', in B. Channakeshava and H.V. Nagaraja Rao (Eds.), *Ananda Bharati: Dr. K Krishnamoorthy Felicitation Volume* (Mysore: D.V.K Murthy, 1995), pp. 151-55.

JAPANESE

793 Dutt, N.V.B.S. *Basic Book of Japanese, Hindi and Telugu* (Delhi: Ajanta Publications, 1995).

- COMPARATIVE LINGUISTICS

794 Kothandaraman, Pon. (Ponnuswamy). *A Comparative Study of Tamil and Japanese* (Madras: International Institute of Tamil Studies, 1994): "Professor G. Devaneya Pavanar Endowment Lecture' no. 7".

795 Lokesh Chandra. 'Tamil Sound-Sequence of the Japanese Alphabet', in Lokesh Chandra, *Cultural Heritage of India* (New Delhi: International Academy of Indian Culture, Aditya Prakashan, 1992), Vol. 2, pp. 211-21.

796 Neustupny, J.V. 'A Note on the Areal Relationship, Between Japanese and Indian Languages', in N.H. Itagi (Ed.), *Spatial Aspects of Language* (Mysore: Central Institute of Indian Languages, 1994), pp. 23-31.

- GRAMMAR AND LEXICON

797 Hikosaka, Shu and Samuel, G. John (Eds.). *A Multilingual Dictionary of Kannada-Kannada-English-Tamil-Japanese* (Madras: Institute of Asian Studies, 1995), Vol. 1 —To be complete in 6 Volumes.

798 Nagarajan, Hemalatha. 'Downslip in Japanese', in Hemalatha Nagarajan, *A Theory of Post-Syntactic Phonology* (Madras: T.R. Publications, 1994), pp. 134-38.

799 Yamashita, K. *Japanese Grammar* (Calcutta: Firma KLM, 1992).

TIBETAN

- GRAMMAR AND LEXICON

800 Chinjor, Pema. *New Plan Tibetan Grammar and Translations* (Bangalore: Pema Chinjor, 1993).

801 Naga, Acharya Sangye T. and Rigzin, Tsepak. *Tibetan Quadrisyllabics, Phrases and Idioms* (Dharamsala: Library of Tibetan Works and Archives, 1994).

802 Rigzin, Tsepak. 'Problems and Suggestions for Making a Tibetan-English Dictionary of Buddhist Terminology', in Doboom Tulku (Ed.), *Buddhist Translations: Problems and*

Perspectives (New Delhi: Manohar Publishers and Distributors, 1995), pp. 138-47.

803 Sen Gupta, Sunil. 'On the Question of Classifiers in Tibetan', in Ashin Dasgupta, *et.al.* (Eds.), *M.M. Vidhusekhar Sastri Commemoration Volume* (Santiniketan: Research Publications, Visva-Bharati, 1990), Vol. 1, pp. 111-18.

- PROVERBS

804 Pemba, Lambo (Com. and Ed.), *Tibetan Proverbs* (Dharamsala: Library of Tibetan Works and Archives, 1996).

- READERS

-- Tibetan-Hindi

805 Sharma, Parmananda, *et.al. Learn to Speak Tibetan and Hindi* (Dharamsala: Library of Tibetan Works and Archives, 1996).

- TRANSLATION

806 Dorjee, Nen Tenzin. 'Styles and Problem Areas in Translating From Tibetan into English', in Doboom Tulku (Ed.), *Buddhist Translations: Problems and Perspectives* (New Delhi: Manohar Publishers and Distributors, 1995), pp. 222-28.

807 Lama Chimpa. 'The Methodology of Translations From Classical Tibetan', in Doboom Tulku (Ed.), *Buddhist Translations: Problems and Perspectives* (New Delhi: Manohar Publishers and Distributors, 1995), pp. 14-9.

808 Mullin, Glann H. 'The Author Versus the Subject as the Focus in Tibetan Translation', in Doboom Tulku (Ed.), *Buddhist Translations: Problems and Perspectives* (New Delhi: Manohar Publishers and Distributors, 1995), pp. 215-21.

809 Pathak, S.K. 'Some Formulae for Translating Buddhist Texts from Tibetan', in Doboom Tulku (Ed.), *Buddhist Translations: Problems and Perspectives* (New Delhi: Manohar Publishers and Distributors, 1995), pp. 43-58.

810 Ruegg, D. Seyfort. 'On Translating Tibetan Philosphical Texts', in Doboom Tulku (Ed.), *Buddhist Translations:*

Problems and Perspectives (New Delhi: Manohar Publishers and Distributors, 1995), pp. 75-86.

811 Wilson, Joe Bransford. 'Problems and Methods in Translation of Buddhist Texts From Tibetan', in Doboom Tulku (Ed.), *Buddhist Translations: Problems and Perspectives* (New Delhi: Manohar Publishers and Distributors, 1995), pp. 148-67.

LAW

- ENVIRONMENTAL LAW

812 Nagore, Arjun Prasad. 'The Japanese Law', in Arjun Prasad Nagore, *Biological Diversity and International Environmental Law* (New Delhi: APH Publishing Corporation, 1996), pp. 208-10.

- FOREIGN TRADE LAW

813 Motiwal, O.P. 'Arbitration in Japan', in O.P. Motiwal and H.K. Awasthi, *International Trade: The Law and Practice* (New Delhi: Bhowmik and Company, 1995), pp. 275-78.

814 Motiwal, O.P. 'Provisional Rules of Procedure of the Foreign Trade Arbitration Commission of China for the Promotion of International Trade', in O.P. Motiwal and H.K. Awasthi, *International Trade: The Law and Practice* (New Delhi: Bhowmik and Company, 1995), pp. 487-92.

- MARITIME

815 Motiwal, O.P. 'The Rules of Maritime Arbitration of the Japan Shipping Exchange, INC', in O.P. Motiwal and H.K. Awasthi, *International Trade: The Law and Practice* (New Delhi: Bhowmik and Company, 1995), pp. 649-72.

LIBRARIES AND BOOKS

- COMPUTERISATION

816 Campbell, Harry. 'Impact of North American On-Line CD-ROM Industry on China', in P.N. Kaula, *et.al.* (Eds.), *International and Comparative Librarianship and Information Systems: Ranganathan Memorial Volumes* (Delhi: B.R. Publishing Corporation, 1996), Vol. 2, pp. 287-92.

LITERATURE

CHINESE

- COMPARATIVE LITERATURE

817 Tan, Chung. 'The Rabindranath Thunder of Oriental Dawn: A Sino-Indian Perspective of Tagore', in Tan Chung (Ed.), *China and India* (New Delhi: Indian Council for Cultural Relations, 1994), pp. 85-107; *Indian Horizons*, Special Issue, Vol. 43, Nos. 1-2, 1994. Reprint from Bhudeb Chaudhuri and K.G. Subrahmanyam (Eds.), *Rabindranath Tagore and the Challenge of Today* (Simla: Indian Institute of Advanced Studies, 1988), pp. 265-85.

- FICTION

818 Saksena, N.S. 'Chinese Invasion', in N.S. Saksena, *Saga of Patriotism and Love: A Historical Novel Dealing with Three Generations of Indians and Russians* (Bareilly: Rohilkhand Publications, 1995), pp. 393-500.

- HISTORY AND CRITICISM

819 Ramachandran, C.N. 'The Concept of Deviation in Sanskrit, Russian and Chinese Formalist Theories: A Note', in B. Channakeshava and H.V. Nagaraja Rao (Eds.), *Ananda Bharati: Dr. K. Krishnamoorthy Felicitation Volume* (Mysore: D.V.K. Murthy, 1995), pp. 357-65.

820 Saikia, Nagen. 'Mao's Literary Views and His Poems', in Girin Phukon and Dhiren Bhagawati (Eds.), *Mao Zedong and Social Reconstruction* (New Delhi: South Asian Publishers, 1996), pp. 175-79.

821 Saran, Vimla. 'Women in Luxunian Literature', in H.S. Gill (Ed.), *Structures of Signification* (New Delhi: Wiley Eastern, 1991), Vol. 2, pp. 344-56.

- POETRY

822 'China', in Krishna Srinivas (Ed.), *World Poetry, 1993: Best Poems by 280 Eminent Poets in 63 Countries* (Madras: World Poetry, 1993), pp. 226-30.

823 Ganguly, Reena. 'Reflection of Chinese Philosophy in Tang Poetry', in Sunil Sen Gupta, Suniti K. Pathak (Eds.),

New Oriental Studies (Santiniketan: Research Publications, Visva-Bharati, 1990), pp. 312-17.

824 Mahapatra, Sitakant. 'Intimacy with the World: Another Look at Poetry During Tang Dynasty', in Tan Chung (Ed.), *China and India* (New Delhi: Indian Council for Cultural Relations, 1994), pp. 427-34; *Indian Horizons*, Special Issue, Vol. 43, Nos. 1-2, 1994.

825 Seth, Vikram. 'Three Chinese Poets: Wang Wei, Li Bai, Du Fu', in Vikram Seth (Tr.), *The Poems, 1981-1994* (New Delhi: Viking, 1995), pp. 215-363.

826 Seth, Vikram (Tr.). Three Chinese Poets: Translations of Poems by Wang Wei, Li Bai, and Du Fu (New Delhi: Viking, 1992).

827 Tan, Chung (Ed.). *Classical Chinese Poetry* (Calcutta: M.P. Birla Foundation, 1991).

828 Wang, Chi-lung (Ed.). 'China and Hongkong', in Krishna Srinivas (Ed.), *World Poetry, 1996: Best Poems by 272 Eminent Poets in 51 Countries* (Madras: World Poetry, 1996), pp. 161-73.

- TRANSLATED LITERATURE

829 Ji, Xianlin. 'Indian Literature in China', in Tan Chung (Ed.), *China and India* (New Delhi: Indian Council for Cultural Relations, 1994), pp. 413-26; *Indian Horizons*, Special Issue, Vol. 43, Nos. 1-2, 1994.

JAPANESE

- DRAMA

830 Ramaswamy, S. 'Seami Motokiyo's Concept of 'Yugen', the Japanese Noh and Sanskrit Drama', in B. Channakeshava and H.V. Nagaraja Rao (Ed.), *Ananda Bharati: Dr. K. Krishnamoorthy Felicitation Volume* (Mysore: D.V.K. Murthy, 1995), pp. 396-407.

- FICTION

831 Morimoto, Tatsuo. 'Genesis of the Japanese Tradition of Narrative Seen in the Genji Monogatari', in Anuja Dev (Ed.), *Narrative: A Seminar Organized by the Sahitya*

Akademi (New Delhi: Sahitya Akademi, 1994), pp. 143-52.

832 Shimazaki, Toson. *Hakai;* tr. into Hindi as *Avajna* (translated title: *Disobedience*) by Savitri Vishwanathan and Anandi Ramnathan (New Delhi: Bharatiya Jnanpith, 1993).

- POETRY

833 Ikeda, Daisaku, *et.al.* 'Japan', in Krishna Srinivas (Ed.), *World Poetry, 1996: Best Poems by 272 Eminent Poets in 51 Countries* (Madras: World Poetry, 1996), pp. 174-98.

834 Sakamura, Shinmin. *Fifteen Selected Poems of Shinmin Sakamura: Transcreated From the Japanese by Hideski Sato* (Calcutta: Writers Workshop, 1994).

835 Srinivas, Krishna (Ed.). *World Poet Ikeda: Seventy World Poets Review 'Poet Ikeda'* (Madras: World Poetry Society, 1994).

PHILOSOPHY AND RELIGION

- BAHAI-ISM

836 Yazdi, Marion. 'From Buddhist to Christian to Bahai', in Annamarie Honnold (Comp. and Ed.), *Why They Bcame Bahais: (First Generation Bahais by 1963)* (New Delhi: Bahai Pub. Trust, 1994), pp. 556-58.

837 Zenimoto, Michitoshi. 'What About My Ancestors", in Annamarie Honnold (Comp. and Ed.), *Why They Bcame Bahais: (First Generation Bahais by 1963)* (New Delhi: Bahai Pub. Trust, 1994), pp. 247-49.

- BUDDHISM

-- Bibliographies and Indexes

838 Sain, G.R. 'Buddhism in Modern World: China', in G.R. Sain, *Buddhist Literature: Yesterday and Today* (Delhi: Concorde Press, 1992), pp. 177-85.

839 Sain, G.R. 'Buddhism in Modern World: Japan', in G.R. Sain, *Buddhist Literature: Yesterday and Today* (Delhi: Concorde Press, 1992), pp. 191-97.

- BUDDHISM

840 Ariyaratne, A.T. 'Sarvodaya Concept of Development and Its Applicability to Building-up an Asian Regional Network Including Japan', in A.T. Ariyanatne, *Buddhism and Sarvodaya: Sri Lankan Experience;* edited by Nandasena Ratnapala (Delhi: Sri Satguru Publications, 1996), pp. 108-32.

841 Bansal, B.L. *Bon, Its Encounter with Buddhism in Tibet* (Delhi: Eastern Book Linkers, 1994).

842 Bhattacharya, Aparna. 'Buddhism in Tibet', in Aparna Bhattacharya, *Sikkim: The Prayer Wheel and Sceptre* (Bombay: Nachiketa Publications, 1994), pp. 32-41.

843 Bru-sgom rGyal-ba g-yung-drung. *The Stages of A. Khrid Meditation: Dzogchen Practice of the Bon Tradition;* tr. by Per Kvaerne and Thupten K. Rikey (Dharamsala: Library of Tibetan Works and Archives, 1996).

844 Chhogdup, Thuptan. 'The Development of Madhyamika Philosophy in Tibet', in Adil Tayyabji, *Indo-Tibetan Madhyamika Studies* (New Delhi: Tibet House; Delhi: Sri Satguru Publications, 1996), pp. 1-14.

845 Dutt, Nalinaksha. 'Expansion of Buddhist Culture in North-East Asia', in D.C. Ahir (Ed.), *A Panorama of Indian Buddhism: Selections From the Maha Bodhi Journal, 1899-1992* (Delhi: Sri Satguru Publications, 1995), pp. 611-23.

846 Franke, Herbert. 'On Chinese Traditions Concerning the Dates of the Buddha', in *When Did the Buddha Live?: The Controversy on the Dating of the Historical Buddha, Selected papers Based on a Symposium Held under the Auspices of the Academy of Sciences in Gottingen* (Delhi: Sri Satguru Publications, 1995), pp. 343-50.

847 Ganguly, Swati. 'Development of Madhyamika Thought in China: A Philosophical Perspective', in Kewal Krishan Mittal (Ed.), *Sunyavada: The Madhyamika Thought* (Delhi: Department of Buddhist Studies, University of Delhi, 1993), pp. 150-56.

848 Ganguly, Swati. 'Development of the Vijnaptimatrata System in India and China', in Swati Ganguly, *Treatise in Thirty Verses on Mere-Consciousness, A Critical English Translation of Hsuan-tsang's Chinese Version of the Vijnaptinatratrimska, with Notes from Dharmapala's*

Commentary in Chinese (Delhi: Motilal Banarsidass Publishers, 1992), pp. 5-17.

849 Ganguly, Swati. 'Life of Hsuan-tsang', in Swati Ganguly, *Treatise in Thirty Verses on Mere-Consciousness, A Critical English Translation of Hsuan-tsang's Chinese Version of the Vijnaptinatratrimska, with Notes from Dharmapala's Commentary in Chinese* (Delhi: Motilal Banarsidass Publishers, 1992), pp. 17-20.

850 Ganguly, Swati. 'Vijnanavada View on the Ten Paramitas in the Cheng Wei-shih-Lun of Husuan Tsang', in Mahesh Tiwary (Ed.), *Perspectives of Buddhist Ethics* (Delhi: Department of Buddhist Studies, University of Delhi, 1991), pp. 108-16.

851 Ganhar, J.N. 'Kashmir and Central Asia: The Buddhist Link', in S. Bhatt (Ed.), *Kashmir Pandits: A Cultural Heritage* (New Delhi: Lancers Books, 1995), pp. 458-62.

852 Gyatso, Tenzin (XIV Dalai Lama). *Commentary on the Thirty Seven Practices of a Bodhisattva*: Nyima Tsering (Tr.), Vyvyan Gayley and Mike Gilmore (Eds.) (Dharamsala: Library of Tibetan Works and Archives, 1995).

853 Kamath, M.V. 'The Spread of Buddhism in China and Japan', in M.V. Kamath, *Letters to Gauri: A Passage to History* (New Delhi: UBS Publishers Distributors, 1996), pp. 134-36.

854 Kapstein, Matthew. *The Dzam-thang Edition of the Collected Works of Kun-mkhyen Dol-po-pa Shes-rab Rgyal-mtshan: Introduction and Catalogue* (Delhi: Shedrup Books, 1992).

855 Krishna Murthy, K. 'Buddhist Philosophy and Symbolism Imbibed in the Scheme of the Tibetan Stupa (MC'ODRTEN) in K. Krishna Murthy, *Studies in Buddhism* (Delhi: Sundeep Prakashan, 1996), pp. 191-98.

856 Krishna Murthy, K. 'China' and 'Japan', in K. Krishna Murthy, *A Dictionary of Buddhist Literature and Literary Personalities* (Delhi: Sundeep Prakashan, 1994), pp. 69-79 and 170-83.

857 Krishna Murthy, K. 'Chinese Buddhism and Buddhist Art', in K. Krishna Murthy, *Studies in Buddhism* (Delhi: Sundeep Prakashan, 1996), pp. 205-12.

858 Kulkarni, S.D. 'China and Central Asia', in S.D. Kulkarni, *India Abroad* (Bombay: Shri Bhagavan Vedavyasa Itihasa Samshodhana Mandira (Bhishma), 1995), pp. 19-26.

859 Lahiri, Latika. 'Lung-Man Cave Inscriptions and the Popularity of Maitreya Bodhisattva', in Kewal Krishan Mittal and Ashvini Agrawal (Eds.), *Buddhist Art and Thought* (New Delhi: Harman Publishing House, 1993), pp. 89-90.

860 Matsunami, Kodo. 'The Significance of Japanese Buddhism', in Hemda Bikash Chowdhury (Ed.), *Jag Jyoti Kripasaran Mahathera 125 Birth Anniversay Volume* (Calcutta: Buddha Dharmankur Sabha, Bengal Buddhist Association, 1990), pp. 51-54.

861 Muling Terahan Gyurmed Dorjee. *The Jewel Ladder: A Preliminary Nyingma Lamrim*: Translated and Edited by Teepak Rigzin (Dharmsala: Library of Tibetan Works and Archives, 1990).

862 Nagender Kumar Singh. *International Encyclopaedia of Buddhism* (New Delhi: Anmol Publications, 1996), Vol. 10-14: Chinese Buddhism.

863 Nakamura, Hajime. 'Japanese Research on the Date of the Buddha', in When Did the Buddha Live?: *The Controversy on the Dating of the Historical Buddha, Selected Papers Based on a Symposium Held under the Auspices of the Academy of Sciences in Gottingen* (Delhi: Sri Satguru Publications, 1995), pp. 135-37.

864 Namkhai, Norbu. *Drung Deu and Bon: Narrations, Symbolic Languages and the Bon Tradition in Ancient Tradition*: Translated from Tibetan into Italian by Adriano Clements, and tr. from Italian into English by Andrew Lukianowiaz (Dharamsala: Library of Tibetan Works and Archives, 1995).

865 Sankarnarayan, Kalpakam and Yorito, Motohiro. 'Concept of Inner Homa in Japanese Shingon Buddhism', in Kalpakam Sankarnarayan, *et.al.* (Eds.),

Buddhism in India and Abroad: An Integrating Influence in Vedic and Post-Vedic Perspective (Mumbai: Somaiya Publications, 1996), pp. 235-38.

866 Sarkar, Anil Kumar. *The Mysteries of Vajrayana Buddhism: From Atisha to Dalai Lama* (New Delhi: South Asian Publishers, 1993).

867 Satchidananda Murty, K. 'Buddho-Taoist Coalescence Under Confucian Auspices', in Tan Chung (Ed.), *China and India* (New Delhi: Indian Council for Cultural Relations, 1994), pp. 225-242; *Indian Horizons*, Special Issue, Vol. 43, Nos. 1-2, 1994.

868 Thakur, Upendra. 'Chinese Monks in India in the Gupta Age', in B.C. Chhabra, *Reappraising Gupta History for S.R. Goyal* (New Delhi: Aditya Prakashan, 1992), pp. 348-57.

869 Yasin, Mohammad and Madhavi. 'Kashmir's Contribution to Chinese Buddhism', in Mohammad Yasin and Madhavi, *Mysteries and Glimpses of Kashmir* (Delhi: Raj Publications, 1996), pp. 57-71.

870 Yuki, Hideo. 'Shinto and Buddhism in Japan', in John S. August (Ed.), *Religious Fundamentalism: An Asian Perspective* (Bangalore: South Asia Theological Research Institute, 1993), pp. 30-44.

871 Zhoo, Puchu. 'Chinese Buddhism—Past and Present', in Hemenda Bikash Chowdhury (Ed.), *Hundred Years of the Bauddha Dharamankur Sabha (The Bengal Buddhist-Association), 1892-1992* (Calcutta: Baudha Dharmankur Sabha, 1993), pp. 135-39.

-- Lamaism

872 Ahir, D.C. 'Tibet', in D.C. Ahir, *Himalayan Buddhism: Past and Present* (Delhi: Sri Satguru Publications, 1993), pp. 205-23.

873 Bhutia, Thinley Dorjey. *Beyond Eternity Through Mysticism* (Darjeeling: Doma Dorji Lhaden, 1994).

874 Dalai Lama. 'Tibetan Buddhism', in Dalai Lama, *The Spirit of The Tibet: Universal Heritage: Selected Speeches and Writings of H.H. The Dalai Lama XIV*, ed. by A.S. Shiromany (New Delhi: Allied, 1995), pp. 333-49.

875 Dalai Lama XIV (Bstan-dzin-rgya-mtsho). *Opening the Mind and Generating a Good Heart*, translated by Tsepak Rigzin and Jeremy Russell (Dharamsala: Library of Tibetan Works and Archives, 1995).

876 Nisha Singh. 'The Initiation Ceremony in Tibetan Monastic Education', in Vijaya Rani and V.K. Goyal (Eds.), *Srijnanamrtam: A Memorial Volume in Honour of Professor Shri Niwas Shastri* (Delhi: Parimal Publications, 1996), pp. 380-83.

877 Rabten, Geshe. *The Preliminary Practices of Tibetan Buddhism*; translated by Gonsar Tulku; compiled by Georges Drussens (New Delhi: Library of Tibetan Works and Archives, 1994).

878 Rinpoche, Khenchen Thrangu. *The Three Vehicles of Buddhist Practice*, tr. by Ken Holmes (Delhi: Sri Satguru Publications, 1995).

879 Shakspo, Nawang Tsering. 'Lamas of Zangskar and the Origin of Tibetan Studies in the West', in Nawang Tsering Shakspo, *Himalayan Buddhist Villages: Environment, Resources, Society and Religious Life in Zangskar, Ladakh* (Delhi: Motilal Banarsidas, 1994), pp. 553-58.

880 Tenzin, Menri Lopon Sangye. *The Twelve Deeds: A Brief Story of Tonpa Shenrab, The Founder of the Bon Religion*; tr. from Tibetan by Sangye Tandar; ed. by Richard Guard (New Delhi: Library of Tibetan Works and Archives, 1995).

-- Zen

881 Ananda. *Zen Buddhist Meditation and Hindu Sadhna: A Comparative and Anthological Study* (New Delhi: APC Publications, 1996).

882 Elkman, Stuart. 'Zen Buddhism', in Stuart Elkman, *The Religions of the World* (Patna: Ramakrishna Mission Ashrama, 1990-91), Vol. 2, pp. 48-53.

883 Limaye, Surekha. 'Patanjali Yoga and Zen', in Kalpakam Sankarnarayan, *et.al.* (Eds.), *Buddhism in India and Abroad: An Integrating Influence in Vedic and Post-Vedic*

Perspective (Mumbai: Somaiya Publications, 1996), pp. 211-17.

884 Limaya, Surekha V. *Zen (Budhism) and Mysticism* (Delhi: Sri Satguru Publications, 1992).

885 Matsuoka, Yukako. 'Zen Buddhism and Fundamentalism', in John S. Augustine (Ed.), *Religious Fundamentalism: An Asian Perspective* (Bangalore: South Asia Theological Research Institute, 1993), pp. 45-52.

886 Mehrotra, Madhu. 'Zen and J.D. Salinger', in R.K. Dhawan (Ed.), *American Literature: New Insights* (New Delhi: Prestige Books, 1995), pp. 21-30.

887 Rajneesh Acharya. *Osho on Zen: Spontaneous Discourses Given by Osho to Disciples and Friends at Osho Commune International, Poona,* Swami Bharat Bharati and Swami Nilambar (Eds.) (New Delhi: New Age International, 1996).

888 Ray, R.N. 'The Development of Zen Doctrine and Its Effect on Japanese Society and Culture', in Barun De, *et.al.* (Eds.), *Proceedings of the Indian History Congress, 56th Session, 1995, Rabindra Bharati University* (Calcutta: Firma KLM, 1996), pp. 907-8.

889 Schadel, Erwin. 'Absolute Nothingness as Selfless Self: Nishtani's Remarks on the Zen-Buddhistic Concept of Reality as a Japanese-Asiatic Contribution to Intercultural Understanding', in Heinrich Beck and Gisela Schmirben (Eds.), *Creative Peace Through Encounter of World Cultures, in Commission of the Hanns Seidel Foundation* (Delhi: Sri Satguru Publications, 1996), pp. 287-312; "Translated from German".

890 Siddharthan, N.S. 'Non-Dualism in Zen Buddhism and Advaita Vedanta', in Kalpakam Sankarnarayan, *et.al.*(Eds.), *Buddhism in India and Abroad: An Integrating Influence in Vedic and Post-Vedic Perspective* (Mumbai: Somaiya Publications, 1996), pp. 218-24.

- CHRISTIANITY

891 Dohi, Akio. 'Christianity in Modern Japan', in T. Dayanandan Francis and F.J. Balasundaram (Eds.), *Asian Expressions of Christian Commitment: A Reader in Asian*

Theology (Madras: Christian Literature Society, 1992), pp. 199-202.

892 D'Souza, Daniel. 'Tibet Mission', in Daniel D'Souza, *Capuchin Missions in India* (Brahmavar, Karnataka: Capuchin Publications, 1993), pp. 33-37.

893 Fida, Ahtisham, *et.al. Jesus Lived in Japan* (Srinagar: Dastgir Publications Trust, 1996).

894 Lee, Peter K.H. 'From Mission to Buddhists to Possibilities of Multi-Faceted Religious Dialogue', in T. Dayanandan Francis and F.J. Balasundaram (Eds.), *Asian Expressions of Christian Commitment: A Reader in Asian Theology* (Madras: Christian Literature Society, 1992), pp. 325-37.

895 Ming, Ng. Lee. 'The Failure of Christianity in China', in T. Dayanandan Francis and F.J. Balasundaram (Eds.), *Asian Expressions of Christian Commitment: A Reader in Asian Theology* (Madras: Christian Literature Society, 1992), pp. 314-18.

896 Tin, John Jyigiokk. 'The Religious Identity in Taiwan', in T. Dayanandan Francis and F.J. Balasundaram (Eds.), *Asian Expressions of Christian Commitment: A Reader in Asian Theology* (Madras: Christian Literature Society, 1992), pp. 319-24.

- CONFUCIANISM

897 Das, Santwana. 'In Chinese Mainland: Confucianism', in Santwana Das, *Theosophy in the Service of World Peace: A Philosophical Study* (Patna: Janaki Prakashan, 1992), pp. 60-76.

898 Fung, Hu-hsiang. 'Confucianism', in Hu-hsiang Fung, *Voices From World Religions, Peace in Our Time*, ed. by Henry O. Thompson (Delhi: Indian Society for Promoting Christian Knowledge, 1993), pp. 153-62.

899 Lee, Cyrus. 'Confucianism', in *The Religions of the World* (Patna: Ramakrishna Mission Ashrama, 1990-91), Vol. 2, pp. 19-28.

900 Sen, Pritam. 'Eastern Philosophies: Confucius and Lao Tzu', in Pritam Sen, *Axiomatic Philosophy* (New Delhi: New Age International, 1996), pp. 181-213.

- PHILOSOPHICAL THOUGHT

901 Chan, W.T. 'The Concept of Man in Chinese Thought', in S. Radhakrishnan and P.T. Raju (Eds.), *The Concept of Man: A Study in Comparative Philosophy* (Delhi: Motilal Banarsidass Publishers, 1992), pp. 172-219.

902 Chi, Lam Shin. 'A Brief History of the Development of Interreligious Relationship in Hong Kong Since 1972', in Henry O. Thompson (Ed.), *World Religions in Dialogue* (Delhi: Indian Society for Promoting Christian Knowledge, 1993), pp. 131-39.

903 Ganguly, Reena. 'Reflection of Chinese Philosophy in Tang Poetry', in Sunil Sen Gupta and Suniti K. Pathak (Eds.), *New Oriental Studies* (Santiniketan: Research Publications, Visva-Bharati, 1990), pp. 312-17.

904 Devadatta, Kanitkar. 'China and Japan', in Kanitkar Devadatta, *Human Life and Cosmic Life* (Pune: Shubhada-Saraswat Prakashan, 1995), pp. 141-76.

905 Kobzev, A.I. 'Murty on Far Eastern Philosophies', in Sibajiban Bhattacharya and Ashok Vohra (Eds.), *The Philosophy of K. Satchidananda Murty* (New Delhi: Indian Council of Philosophical Research, 1995), pp. 272-83.

906 Kobzev, A.I. 'Professor Murty's Understanding of Chinese Philosophy', in Tan Chung (Ed.), *China and India* (New Delhi: Indian Council for Cultural Relations, 1994), pp. 243-47; *Indian Horizons*, Special Issue, Vol. 43, Nos. 1-2, 1994.

907 Pande, G.C. 'Reflections on the Classic Chinese Vision of Man', in Tan Chung (Ed.), *China and India* (New Delhi: Indian Council for Cultural Relations, 1994), pp. 249-53; *Indian Horizons*, Special Issue, Vol. 43, Nos. 1-2, 1994.

- RELIGIOUS SITUATION

908 Kelsang, Ladrang. *The Guardian Deities of Tibet*; tr. from Tibetan by Pema Thinley (Dharamsala: Little Lhasa Publications; New Delhi: Distribution Paljor Publications, 1996) .

- SHINTOISM

909 Batumalai, S. 'An Introduction to Japanese Theological Thinking', in S. Batamalai, *An Introduction to Asian*

Theology: An Asian Story From a Malaysian Eye for Asian Neighbourology (Delhi: ISPCK, 1991), pp. 88-115.

910 Gupta, N.L. 'Shintoism: Japanese Version of Taoism and Religion in Japan', in N.L. Gupta, *An Introduction to Equality of Religions* (New Delhi: Mohit Publications, 1996), pp. 59-64.

911 Satyalokananda. 'Shintoism', in Satyalokananda, *The Religions of World* (Patna: Ramakrishna Mission Ashrama, 1990-91), Vol. 2, pp. 54-59.

- TAOISM

912 Choudhuri, Indra Nath. 'Indian Response to the Book of Tao', in Tan Chung (Ed.), *China and India* (New Delhi: Indian Council for Cultural Relations, 1994), pp. 435-42; *Indian Horizons*, Special Issue, Vol. 43, Nos. 1-2, 1994.

913 Lee, Cyrus. 'Taoism', in Cyrus Lee, *The Religions of the World* (Patna: Ramakrishna Mission Ashrama, 1990-91), Vol. 2, pp. 29-37.

914 Limaye, Surekha V. 'Taoism of Lao-Tzu and Chuang-Tze', in Surekha V. Limaye, *Zen (Buddhism) and Mysticism* (Delhi: Sri Satguru Publications, 1992), pp. 27-32.

915 Panakal, Justin. 'Taoism', in Justin Panakal, *Blossoms of Carmel* (Alwaye: Pontifical Institute Publications, 1995), pp. 113, 123.

916 Raghu Vira. *Tibetan Mandals: Vajravali and Tantra-Samuccaya* (New Delhi: International Academy of Indian Culture, 1995).

POLITICS AND GOVERNMENT

- CONSTITUTION AND CONSTITUTIONALISM

917 Bhattacharya, Pranab. *The Japanese Constitution: A Study* (Calcutta: Progressive Publishers, 1993).

- LEGISLATURE

918 Jain, C.K. 'Japan', in C.K. Jain (Ed.), *Triumph of Democracy: An Overview of World Parliaments* (New Delhi:

Lok Sabha Secretriat; CBS Publishers and Distributors, 1993), pp. 805-08.

919 Robinson, Donald L. 'Why Americans Chose Parliamentary Government for Japan', in Subrata Mukherjee and Sushila Ramaswamy (Eds.), *Issues in Comparative Politics* (New Delhi: Deep and Deep Publications, 1996), pp. 170-93.

- POLITICAL FREEDOM

920 Fang, Li-zhi. 'Human Rights in China', in Arun Gandhi (Ed.), *World Without Violence: Can Gandhi's Vision Become Reality* (New Delhi: Wiley Eastern, 1994), pp. 148-49.

921 Mohanty, Manorajan. 'Swaraj and Jiefang: Freedom Discourse in India and China', in Neera Chandok (Ed.), *Understanding the Post-Colonial World : Theory and Method* (New Delhi: Sterling Publishers, 1994), pp. 104-09.

922 Sorman, Guy. 'The Fifth Modernisation', in Guy Sorman, *The Unborn Revolution*: translated from the French by Asha Puri (New Delhi: Vikas Publishing House, 1991), pp. 280-86.

923 Sorman, Guy. 'Looking Back on Tiananmen', in Guy Sorman, *The Unborn Revolution*: translated from the French by Asha Puri (New Delhi: Vikas Publishing House, 1991), pp. 269-79 .

924 Sorman, Guy. 'The Wall of Democracy', in Guy Sorman, *The Unborn Revolution*: translated from the French by Asha Puri (New Delhi: Vikas Publishing House, 1991), pp. 237-38.

925 True, Michael. 'The 1989 Democratic Uprising in China: A Nonviolent Perspective', in Mahendra Kumar (Ed.), *Legacy and Future of Nonviolence* (New Delhi: Gandhi Peace Foundation, 1996), pp. 141-57.

- POLITICAL IDEOLOGY

926 Astafyev, G. 'The Distinctive Features of the System of Chinese People's Democracy', in Anil Biswas and Anjan Bera (Eds.), *Democracy and Marxism (Collection of Articles and Documents)* (Calcutta: National Book Agency, 1993), pp. 65-76.

926A Bhaduri, Ashok. 'Mao Ze Dong on Intellectuals', in Ashok Bhaduri, *Gramsie and the Intellectuals: A Critical Study* (Calcutta: Ratna Prakashan, 1995), pp. 36-42.

927 Bhagawati, Dhiren. 'Mao's Contributions to Marxian Epistemology', in Girin Phukon and Dhiren Bhagawati (Eds.), *Mao Zedong and Social Reconstruction* (New Delhi: South Asian Publishers, 1996), pp. 43-49.

928 Bhattacharjea, Mira Sinha. 'China: Ploughing a Lonely Furrow', in Sushil Kumar (Ed.), *Gorbachev's Reforms and International Change* (New Delhi: Lancers Books, 1993), pp. 136-53.

929 Bhattacharjea, Mira Sinha. 'Gandhi and Mao—A Search for Similarities', in Tan Chung (Ed.), *China and India* (New Delhi: Indian Council for Cultural Relations, 1994), pp. 255-64; *Indian Horizons*, Special Issue, Vol. 43, Nos. 1-2, 1994.

930 Bhattacharyya, Budhadeva. 'New Democracy: Its Role and Limits', in Girin Phukon and Dhiren Bhagawati (Eds.), *Mao Zedong and Social Reconstruction* (New Delhi: South Asian Publishers, 1996), pp. 58-68.

931 Bose, Pradip. 'Aspects of Maoism and its Impact on India', in Pradip Bose, *Communism and Communist Systems: Some Reflections* (New Delhi: Deep and Deep Publications, 1995), pp. 285-98.

932 Bose, Pradip. 'Democratic Socialism Versus Maoism', in Pradip Bose, *Communism and Communist Systems: Some Reflections* (New Delhi: Deep and Deep Publications, 1995), pp. 407-11.

933 Bose, Pradip. 'Prospects for Chinese Communism in the 1990s', in Pradip Bose, *Communism and Communist Systems: Some Reflections* (New Delhi: Deep and Deep Publications, 1995), pp. 334-41.

934 Chao, Yang. 'Conscientiously Study Chairman Mao's Theory of Continuing the Revolution Under the Dictatorship of the Proletariat', in Suniti Kumar Ghosh (Ed.), *The Historic Turning Point: A Liberation Anthology* (Calcutta: S.K. Ghosh, 1993), Vol. 2, pp. 155-56: "*From Liberation*, Vol. 3, No. 3, March 1970."

935 'Comments of Comrade Chou En-lai and Comrade Kang Sheng on the Party Line', in Suniti Kumar Ghosh (Ed.), *The Historic Turning Point: A Liberation Anthology* (Calcutta: S.K. Ghosh, 1993), Vol. 2, pp. 331-38. "A Report of the Interview Souren Bose had with Chou En-lai and Kang Sheng in Peking on 29 October 1970."

936 'CPC 14th Congress Document' (Excerpts of the Political Report to the 14th Congress of the CPC, held in October 1992), in Anil Biswas and Anjan Bera (Eds.), *Democracy and Marxism: Collection of Articles and Documents* (Calcutta: National Book Agency, 1993), pp. 375-83 .

937 Hussain, Maqitul. 'Mao's Practice: A Sociology of Knowledge Interpretation', in Girin Phukon and Dhiren Bhagawati (Eds.), *Mao Zedong and Social Reconstruction* (New Delhi: South Asian Publishers, 1996), pp. 97-102.

938 Kagalkar, P.C. 'Chinese Socialism', in P.C. Kagalkar, *Renaissance of Democratic Concepts on Global Scene and Collapse of Socialism: A Comparative Study of Socialism and Democracy* (Bombay: Himalaya Publishing House, 1996), pp. 40-42.

939 Majumdar, Charu. 'China's Chairman is Our Chairman: China's Path is Our Path', in Suniti Kumar Ghosh (Ed.), *The Historic Turning Point: A Liberation Anthology* (Calcutta: S.K. Ghosh, 1993), Vol. 2, pp. 45-51. "*From Liberation*, Vol. 3, No. 1, November 1969."

940 Misra, Tilottoma. 'Influence of Mao's Thought on the Indian Students (1967-71): Looking Back', in Girin Phukon and Dhiren Bhagawati (Eds.), *Mao Zedong and Social Reconstruction* (New Delhi: South Asian Publishers, 1996), pp. 149-63.

941 Mohanty, Manoranjan. 'Power of History: Mao Zedong Thought and Deng's China', in Girin Phukon and Dhiren Bhagawati (Eds.), *Mao Zedong and Social Reconstruction* (New Delhi: South Asian Publishers, 1996), pp. 12-24.

942 Phukon, Girin. 'Dialects of Scientific Socialism: A Study of Mao's "On Contradiction"', in Girin Phukon and Dhiren Bhagawati (Eds.), *Mao Zedong and Social*

Reconstruction (New Delhi: South Asian Publishers, 1996), pp. 25-42.

943 Phukon, Girin and Bhagawati, Dhiren (Eds.), *Mao Zedong and Social Reconstruction* (New Delhi: South Asian Publishers, 1996). "Based on the Presentation Made at a National Seminar Organized by the Department of Political Science, Dibrugarh University, 1994."

944 Purushothaman, E.N. 'China', in E.N. Purushothaman, *Communism is Humanism* (Hyderabad: Andhra Pradesh Police Academy, 1995), pp. 160-72.

945 Ramaswamy, Sushila. 'Non-Traditional views on State: Mao and Euro-Communists', in Sushila Ramaswamy, *Marxist Theory of the State: Dictatorship of the Proletariat* (New Delhi: Deep and Deep Publications, 1993), pp. 125-42.

946 Ray, Ashish K. 'Marxism, Mao Zedong and the Concept of Peasant Communism', in Girin Phukon and Dhiren Bhagawati (Eds.), *Mao Zedong and Social Reconstruction* (New Delhi: South Asian Publishers, 1996), pp. 69-84.

947 Roy, Ajit. *On Marxist Theory and Practice: From Stalin and Mao to Gorbachev and Deng* (Calcutta: Marxist Review, 1992).

948 Roy, Himanshu. 'Will Communist China Survive?', in Himanshu Roy, *Critique of Leninism* (Calcutta: Semaphore Publishers, 1994), pp. 104-23.

949 Sarkar, Sunil Kumar. 'The Fall of China', in Sunil Kumar Sarkar, *The Rise and Fall of Communism* (New Delhi: Atlantic Publishers and Distributors, 1994), pp. 99-111.

950 Sen Gupta, Asin Kumar. 'The China Phenomenon' in Asim Sen, *Socialism Versus Capitalism in the 1990s* (Calcutta: Management Science Publication, 1994), pp. 121-31.

951 Sorman, Guy. 'Contract Socialism', in Guy Sorman, *The Unborn Revolution*: translated from the French by Asha Puri (New Delhi: Vikas Publishing House, 1991), pp. 258-68.

952 Sorman, Guy. 'A Prayer for Mao', in Guy Sorman, *The Unborn Revolution*: translated from the French by Asha

Puri (New Delhi: Vikas Publishing House, 1991), pp. 287-92.

953 Sorman, Guy. 'The Three Lives of Yan Hansheng', in Guy Sorman, *The Unborn Revolution*: translated from the French by Asha Puri (New Delhi: Vikas Publishing House, 1991), pp. 247-57.

954 Thomson, George. 'Marxism in China Today', in Suniti Kumar Ghosh (Ed.), *The Historic Turning Point: A Liberation Anthology* (Calcutta: S.K. Ghosh, 1992), Vol. 1, pp. 239-55.

955 Tsai, Cheng. 'Our Country is Now Socialist Country Without Internal or External Debts', in Suniti Kumar Ghosh (Ed.), *The Historic Turning Point: A Liberation Anthology* (Calcutta: S.K. Ghosh, 1992), Vol. 1, pp. 258-63.

956 Yan, Ling. 'The Transformation From New Democracy to Socialism', in Anil Biswas and Anjan Bera (Eds.), *Democracy and Marxism: Collection of Articles and Documents* (Calcutta: National Book Agency, 1993), pp. 77-123.

- POLITICAL LEADERSHIP

957 Bepin Behari. 'Dalai Lama', in Bepin Behari, *Astrological Biographies: Seventeen Examples of Predictive Insights* (Delhi: Motilal Banarsidass Publishers, 1996), pp. 99-140.

958 Bhatia, L.M. 'Modern China's First Premier', in L.M. Bhatia, *Reflections on Political Personages and Other Topics* (New Delhi: Reliance Publishing House, 1996), pp. 117-22.

959 Bhattacharyya, A.K. *President Chiang Kai-shek: The World Leader* (Calcutta: Firma KLM, 1990).

960 Hussain, T. Karki, 'Deng Xiaoping: A Political Profile', in Bibek Debroy (Ed.), *China's External Trade Since the Reforms* (New Delhi: Commonwealth Publishers, 1991), pp. 15-30.

961 Sahu, Surendra. 'Mao Tse-tung', in Surendra Sahu, *One Hundred Lives of Genius* (Calcutta: Writers Workshop, 1994), pp. 112-19.

962 Tsai, Cheng. 'The Bankruptcy of China's Devotees of Parliament', in Suniti Kumar Ghosh (Ed.), *The Historic*

Turning Point: A Liberation Anthology (Calcutta: S.K. Ghosh, 1992), Vol. 1, pp. 232-39.

- POLITICAL PARTIES

963 Hirose, Takako. *Two Asian Democracies: A Comparative Study of the Single Predominant Party Systems of India and Japan* (New Delhi: Konark Publishers, 1993).

964 Lu, Yun. 'Multi-Party Cooperation in China', in Anil Biswas and Anjan Bera (Eds.), *Democracy and Marxism: Collection of Articles and Documents* (Calcutta: National Book Agency, 1993), pp. 366-74.

965 Namboodiripad, E.M.S. 'The Naxalites and the Chinese Party', in E.M.S. Namboodiripad, *The Communist Party in Kerala: Six Decades of Struggle and Advance* (New Delhi: National Book Centre, 1995), pp. 231-36.

966 Seldon, Mark. 'The Chinese Communist Party and the Countryside: Reflections on Method', in R.K. Bhattacharya, *et.al.* (Eds.), *Sociology in the Rubric of Social Science: Professor Ramkrishna Mukherjee Felicitation Volume* (Calcutta: Anthropological Survey of India, Ministry of Human Resource Development, Department of Culture, Government of India, 1995), pp. 131-45.

967 Sorman, Guy. 'The Last Days of the Chinese Communist Party', in Guy Sorman, *The Unborn Revolution*: translated from the French by Asha Puri (New Delhi: Vikas Publishing House, 1991), pp. 239-46.

- POLITICAL SITUATION

968 'C.C. Resolution on Developments in People's China Adopted on July 15-17, 1989', in *In Defence of Marxism-Leninism: A Collection of CPI(M) Documents, May '88 to August 1991* (New Delhi: Communist Party of India (M), 1991), pp. 40-56.

969 Krishnaswami, N. *Know Japan: Know the Japanese* (Madras: T.R. Publications, 1996). "A Collection of the author's articles published in *The Hindu*, 1991-95."

970 *Present Conditions in Tibet* (Dharamsala: Office of Information and International Relations, 1990).

- POLITICAL STRUCTURE

971 Bedeski, Robert. 'Sssuma Chien and the Notion of the State', in V. Subramaniam (Ed.), *Political Theorizing in Asia: The Socio-Cultural Context* (Delhi: Ajanta Publications, 1994), pp. 154-72.

- POLITICAL THOUGHT

972 Bedeski, Robert. 'Political Thought in Ancient China: Sssuma Chien and the Notion of the State', in V. Subramaniam (Ed.), *Political Theorizing in Asia: The Socio-Cultural Context* (Delhi: Ajanta Publications, 1994), pp. 154-72.

973 Mittal, Nemi Sharan. *Confucian Political Thinkers and Thought* (Jaipur: Printwell, 1995).

974 Subramaniam, V. 'Intellectuals in State and Society in India and China: Some Critical Comparisons', in V. Subramaniam (Ed.), *Political Theorizing in Asia: The Socio-Cultural Context* (Delhi: Ajanta Publications, 1994), pp. 1-19.

- PUBLIC ADMINISTRATION

975 Cao, Guoying and Zhang, Houan. 'The Villagers' Self-Government in Lishu County, Jilin Province, of the People's Republic of China', in Abdul Aziz and David D. Arnold (Eds.), *Decentralised Governance in Asian Countries* (New Delhi: Sage Publications, 1996), pp. 104-24.

976 Mathew, George. 'The Chinese Experiment with Local Self-Government', in George Mathew, *Panchayati Raj: From Legislation to Movement* (New Delhi: Concept Publishing Company, 1994), pp. 87-102.

977 Mathur, B.C. 'Training of Civil Servants in Japan', in Raimann Pattanayak (Ed.), *Training for Organizational Development* (New Delhi: Anmol Publications, 1994), pp. 259-83.

978 Meenakshisundaram, S.S. 'Chinese Form of Local Governments', in S.S. Meenakshisundaram, *Decentralization in Developing Countries* (New Delhi: Concept Publishing Company, 1994), pp. 36-54.

979 Wang, Zhenyo. 'Chinese Village Autonomy: Present Status and Future Prospects', in Abdul Aziz and David D. Arnold (Eds.), *Decentralised Governance in Asian Countries* (New Delhi: Sage Publications, 1996), pp. 82-103.

980 Zhang, Jinggan. 'The Development and Problems of Water Supply and Sanitation in the Past 42 Years in Beijing', in Bidyut Mohanty (Ed.), *Urbanisation in Developing Countries: Basic Services and Community Participation* (New Delhi: Concept Publishing Company, 1993), pp. 65-73.

- REGIONAL/PERIPHERAL ISSUES

-- Hong Kong

981 Gage, Robert W. 'Regionalization in China and Their Implications in Hong Kong', in Pradeep K. Saxena, *Changing States and Bureaucracy* (Jaipur: RBSA Publishers, 1996), pp. 73-96.

982 Lan-Kam-Sang. 'The Structure and Organization of the Legislative Council in Hong Kong', in *Commonwealth Parliaments: A Commemorative Souvenir, 37th Commonwealth Parliamentary Conference, New Delhi, September 1991* (New Delhi: Lok Sabha Secretariat for the Indian Parliamentary Group, 1991), pp. 80-110.

-- Taiwan

983 Hsieh, John Fuh-sheng, 'Parliamentarianism Versus Presidentialism: The Politics of Constitutional Reforms in the Republic of China or Taiwan', in Subrata Mukherjee and Sushila Ramaswamy (Eds.), *Issues in Comparative Politics* (New Delhi: Deep and Deep Publications, 1996), pp. 151-69.

-- Tibet

984 Anand Kumar (Ed.), *Tibet: A Sourcebook* (New Delhi: Radiant Publishers, 1995).

985 Chitkara, M.G. *Tibet: A Reality* (New Delhi: Ashish Publishing House, 1994).

986 Chitkara, M.G. *Toxic Tibet Under Nuclear China* (New Delhi: APH Publishing Corporation, 1996).

987 Dalai Lama. *His Holiness the Dalai Lama: Speeches, Statements, Articles, Interviews, 1987 to June 1995* (Dharamsala: Department of Information and International Relations, Central Tibetan Administration, 1995).

988 Dalai Lama, 'Sino-Tibetan Relations (Five Points Peace Plan)' in Dalai Lama. *The Spirit of the Tibet: Universal Heritage: Selected Speeches and Writings of H.H. the Dalai Lama XIV*, edited by A.A.Shiromany (New Delhi: Allied, 1995), pp. 151-90.

989 Dalai Lama. *The Spirit of Tibet: Universal Heritage: Selected Speeches and Writings of HH the Dalai Lama XIV*, A.A. Shiromany (Ed.) (New Delhi: Allied, 1995).

990 Dalai Lama XIV. *The Spirit of Tibet: Vision for Human Liberation: Selected Speeches and Writings of H.H. The XIV Dalai*, A.A. Shiromany (Ed.) (New Delhi: Tibetan Parliamentary and Policy Research Centre and Vikas Publishing House, 1996). "Companion Volume to: *The Spirit of Tibet: Universal Heritage: Selected Speeches and Writings of H.H. The Dalai Lama XIV*."

991 Doig, Desmond. 'Tibet, Under My Skin', in Desmond Doig, *Look Back in Wonder* (New Delhi: Indus, Harper-Collins Publishers, 1995), pp. 219-25.

992 Gautier, Francsis. 'China', in Francsis Gautier, *Rewriting Indian History* (Delhi: Vikas Publishing House, 1996), pp. 118-20.

993 Jagat Singh (Bright). *Why China Must Quit Tibet* (New Delhi: Omsons Publications, 1994).

994 Kler, Gurdip. 'Tibet', in Gurdip Singh Kler, *Unsung Battles of 1962* (New Delhi: Lancer Publishers and Distributors, 1995), pp. 47-90.

995 Kleteger, P. Christian. *Tibetan Nationalism: The Role of Patronage in the Accomplishment of a National Identity* (Meerut: Archana Publications, 1992).

996 Nehru, Jawaharlal. 'Nehru's Statement in Lok Sabha on the Situation in Tibet, New Delhi, April 27, 1959', in Dalai Lama, *The Spirit of the Tibet, Universal Heritage: Selected Speeches and Writings of H.H. The Dalai Lama XIV*,

A.A. Shiromany (Ed.) (New Delhi: Allied, 1995), pp. 353-60.

997 Pathak, Suniti K. 'Modern Tibetan Studies in India', in Sunil Sen Gupta and Suniti K. Pathak (Eds.), *New Oriental Studies* (Santiniketan: Research Publications, Visva Bharati, 1990), pp. 289-94.

998 Ram Rahul, 'Governance of Tibet', in Ram Rahul, *Central Asia: Major Perspectives* (New Delhi: Vikas, 1993), pp. 1-25.

999 Ram Rahul. 'Tibet', in Ram Rahul, *Central Asia: Major Perspectives* (New Delhi: Vikas, 1993), pp. 14-51.

1000 Sharma, Parmananda. 'The Status of Tibet: A Historical Perspective', in M.G. Chitkara, *Toxic Tibet Under Nuclear China* (New Delhi : APH Publishing Corporation, 1996), pp. 131-35.

1001 *Tibet: Proving Truth From Dharamsala* (Department of Information and International Relations, Central Tibetan Administration of H.H. the Dalai Lama, 1993).

1002 Vajpayee, Atal Bihari. 'Tibet', in Atal Bihari Vajpayee, *Four Decades in Parliament*, N.M. Ghatate (Ed.) (Delhi: Shipra Publications, 1996), Vol. 3, *Foreign Affairs*, pp. 159-69.

1003 Vatsayan, Kapila. 'An Interview with His Holiness, The Dalai Lama', in Ramesh Chandra Tewari and Krishna Nath (Eds.), *Universal Responsibility: A Felicitation Volume in Honour of His Holiness the Fourteenth Dalai Lama, Tenzin Gyatso, on His Sixteenth Birthday* (New Delhi: Foundation for Universal Responsibility of His Holiness the Dalai Lama: ANB Publishers, 1996), pp. 251-57.

-- Xinjiang

1004 Ram Rahul. 'Xinjiang', in Ram Rahul, *Central Asia: Major Perspectives* (New Delhi: Vikas, 1993), pp. 52-86.

- REVOLUTIONS AND REVOLUTIONARY IDEAS

1005 Chen, Zhihua. 'The United Front Experience in Russia and China', in Manoranjan Mohanty (Ed.), *Chinese Revolution: Comparative Perspectives on Transformation of*

Non-Western Societies (Delhi: Ajanta Publications, 1992), pp. 261-72.

1006 Ghosh, Suniti Kumar. 'Fight Self-Interest', in Suniti Kumar Ghosh (Ed.), *The Historic Turning Point: A Liberation Anthology* (Calcutta: S.K. Gosh, 1992), Vol. 1, pp. 255-58.

1007 Ghosh, Suniti Kumar. 'On China's Proletarian Cultural Revolution', in Suniti Kumar Ghosh (Ed.), *The Historic Turning Point: A Liberation Anthology* (Calcutta: S.K. Gosh, 1992), Vol. 1, pp. 36-37.

1008 Gong, Shuduo. 'Chinese Revolution and Culture', in Manoranjan Mohanty (Ed.), *Chinese Revolution: Comparative Perspectives on Transformation of Non-Western Societies* (Delhi: Ajanta Publications, 1992), pp. 95-114.

1009 Li, Zhongying. 'The National People's Congress of the People's Republic of China', in C.K.Jain (Ed.), *Triumph of Democracy: An Overview of World Parliaments* (New Delhi: Lok Sabha Secretariat, CBS Publishers and Distributors, 1993), pp. 284-89.

1010 Mohanty, Manoranjan (Ed.), *Chinese Revolution: Comparative Perspectives on Transformation of Non-Western Societies* (Delhi: Ajanta Publications, 1992). "Papers presented at the International Conference on Social Transformation in Modern China, held at Mangzhou in November 1987."

1011 Mohanty, Manoranjan. The Chinese Revolution: Reconsiderations in Revolutionary Theory', in Manoranjan Mohanty (Ed.), *Chinese Revolution: Comparative Perspectives on Transformation of Non-Western Societies* (Delhi: Ajanta Publications, 1992), pp. 3-28.

1012 Mohanty, Manoranjan. 'The Dynamics of the Internal and the External in the Chinese and Russian Revolution', in Manoranjan Mohanty (Ed.), *Chinese Revolution: Comparative Perspectives on Transformation of Non-Western Societies* (Delhi: Ajanta Publications, 1992), pp. 273-88.

1013 Romero-Castilla, Abfredo. 'Capitalist State Competition vs. National Sovereignty: Meiji Ishin, Chinese and Mexican Revolutions', in Manoranjan Mohanty (Ed.), *Chinese Revolution: Comparative Perspectives on*

Transformation of Non-Western Societies (Delhi: Ajanta Publications, 1992), pp. 201-33.

1014 Shanti Swarup. 'Carrying the Revolution to Reconsideration: Mao's Dilemma', in Girin Phukon and Dhiren Bhagawati (Eds.), *Mao Zedong and Social Reconstruction* (New Delhi: South Asian Publishers, 1996), pp. 50-57.

1015 Wang, Qingcheng. 'China's Modernization and Political Revolution', in Manoranjan Mohanty (Ed.), *Chinese Revolution: Comparative Perspectives on Transformation of Non-Western Societies* (Delhi: Ajanta Publications, 1992), pp. 29-32.

1016 Yamaguchi Ichiro. 'The Meiji Restoration and the Chinese Revolution', in Manoranjan Mohanty (Ed.), *Chinese Revolution: Comparative Perspectives on Transformation of Non-Western Societies* (Delhi: Ajanta Publications, 1992), pp. 187-99.

PSYCHOLOGY

1017 Mishra, Bharat. 'First Blind Professor in Japan', in Bharat Mishra, *Eminent Blind Persons of the World* (New Delhi: Ashish Publishing House, 1992), pp. 1-3.

1018 Mishra, Bharat. 'Takeo Iwahashi—A Blind Social Worker of Japan', in Bharat Mishra, *Eminent Blind Persons of the World* (New Delhi: Ashish Publishing House, 1992), pp. 4-7.

1019 Cheng, Christopher H.K. 'Towards a Culturally Relevant Model of Self-Concept for the Hong Kong Chinese', in Janak Pandey, *et.al.* (Eds.), *Asian Contributions to Cross-Cultural Psychology* (New Delhi: Sage Publications, 1996), pp. 235-54.

1020 Feather, N.T. and Mckee, I.R. 'Global Self-esteem and the Fall of High Achievers: Australian and Japanese Comparisons', in Janak Pandey, *et.al.* (Eds.), *Asian Contributions to Cross-Cultural Psychology* (New Delhi: Sage Publications, 1996), pp. 200-13.

1021 Gudykunst, William B., *et.al.* 'Self-Monitoring and Concern for Social Appropriateness in China and England', in Janak Pandey, *et.al.* (Eds.), *Asian*

Contributions to Cross-Cultural Psychology (New Delhi: Sage Publications, 1996), pp. 255-67.

SCIENCE AND TECHNOLOGY

1022 Alvares, Claude. 'Chinese Technology and Culture: 1368-1842', in Claude Alvares, *Decolonizing History: Technology and Culture in India, China and the West 1492 to the Present Day* (Goa: Other India Press, 1991), pp. 75-107.

1023 Kharbanda, V.P. 'China', in A. Rehman (Ed.), *Science, Technology and Development* (New Delhi: New Age International Publishers, Wiley Eastern, 1995), pp. 179-220.

1024 Lancaster, F.W. 'Some Publication Patterns in Indian and Japanese Science: A Bibliometric Comparison', in B.M. Gupta (Ed.), *Handbook of Libraries, Archives and Information Centres in India* (New Delhi: Segment Books, 1996), Vol. 5, pp. 36-49.

1025 Sondha, Sunil. 'Japan', in A. Rehman (Ed.), *Science, Technology and Development* (New Delhi: New Age International Publishers, Wiley Eastern, 1995), pp. 152-78.

1026 Tomitate, Takao. 'Japanese Technology Transfer Policy and Problems in Future', in R.K. Pachauri, *et.al.* (Eds.), *Climate Change in Asia and Brazil: The Role of Technology Transfer* (New Delhi: Tata Energy Research Institute, 1994), pp. 111-17.

1027 Wu, Zongxin. 'Technology Development of Cogeneration and Energy Saving Lighting in China: An Overview', in R.K. Pachauri, *et.al.* (Eds.), *Climate Change in Asia and Brazil: The Role of Technology Transfer* (New Delhi: Tata Energy Research Institute, 1994), pp. 165-71.

- AGRICULTURAL SCIENCES

1028 Zhang, Xinhui. 'Chinese Women in Science and Technology', in Devalina Kohli (Ed.), *Report of Asian and Pacific Consultation of Non-Governmental Organisations on Women in Development, April 1994, India International*

Centre (New Delhi: All India Women Conference, 1994), p. 37.

1029 Chen, Jiaju. 'Present Status of Foxtail Millet and Proso Millet Genetic Resources Conservaton in China', in K.W. Riley, *et.al.* (Eds.), *Advances in Small Millets* (New Delhi: Oxford and IBH Publishing Company, 1993), pp. 401-8.

1030 Chen, Jiaju. 'Recent Development in Foxtail Millet Cultivation and Research in China' in K.W.Riley, *et.al.* (Eds.), *Advances in Small Millets* (New Delhi: Oxford and IBH Pub. Company, 1993), pp. 101-7.

1031 Chen, Y., *et.al.* 'The Use of Yield Increasing Bacteria (YIB) as Plant Growth Promoting Rhizobacteria in Chinese Agriculture', in R.S. Utkhede (Ed.), *Management of Soil Borne Diseases* (Ludhiana: Kalyani Publishers, 1996), pp. 164-84.

1032 Chiou, Robin Y.Y. 'Status of Agro-Food Industries in Taiwan', in C.P. Natarajan and S. Ranganna (Eds.), *Trends in Food Science and Technology: Proceedings of the Third International Food Convention (IFCON '93), held During 7th to 12th September 1993 at Mysore* (Mysore: Association of Food Scientists and Technologists, 1995), pp. 54-57.

1033 Huo, Yongkang and Shi, Xien. 'Progress and Prospect of Tropical Sericulture in South China', in A.K. Ganguly (Ed.), *Global Silk Scenario-2001: Proceedings of the International Conference on Sericulture, 94* (New Delhi: Oxford and IBH Publishing Company, 1996), pp. 207-13.

1034 Sapai, Tetsuo. 'Apis Cerana Beekeeping in Japan', in L.R. Verma (Ed.), in *Honeybees in Mountain Agriculture* (New Delhi: Oxford and IBH, 1992), pp. 135-238.

- ASTRONOMY

1035 Tan, Chung. 'Chinese Cosmogony: Man-nature Synthesis', in Kapila Vatsayan (Ed.), *Prakrti: The Integral Vision* (New Delhi: Indira Gandhi National Centre for the Arts, D.K. Print World, 1995), pp. 15-27.

1035A *Tashi, T. Tibetan Astronomy, Astrology: A Brief Introduction* (Dharamsala:. Gangchen Kyishong, Astro Department, 1995).

- BIOLOGY

1036 Jin, Zhen-Ming. 'The Advancement of Agricultural Science and Technology in China', in L.R. Verma (Ed.), *Honeybees in Mountain Agriculture* (New Delhi: Oxford and IBH, 1992), pp. 133-47.

1037 Sugahara, T. 'Hiroshima and Nagasaki: From Fear Through Science to Risk Assessment', in D.D. Sood, *et.al.* (Eds.), *RON-BEC 100: Proceedings of the International Conference: Hundred Years of X-Rays and Radioactivity, 1996, Bhabha Atomic Research Centre, Mumbai, India* (Mumbai: Library and Information Services Division, BARC, 1996), pp. 367-76.

- BOTANY

1038 Chung, Hsu-Ho and Lee, Jovial Y.C. 'Diseases of Forest Trees and Their Control in Taiwan', S.P. Raychaudhri and Karl Maramorosch (Eds.), *Forest Trees and Palms: Diseases and Control* (New Delhi: Oxford and IBH Publishing Company, 1996), pp. 81-93.

1039 Haigh, Martin J. 'Agrobotanic Research Among the Shifting Cultivators of Xishungbanna Southwest China: Lessons for the Himalaya', in D.C. Pande (Ed.), *Dimensions of Agriculture in the Himalaya* (Almora: Shri Almora Book Depot, 1996), pp. 89-95.

1040 Kachroo, P. 'Sino-Japanese-Himalayan Perspective', in P. Kachroo, *Central Asia and Kashmir: Archaeobotany and Floristics* (Jodhpur: Scientific Publishers, 1995), pp. 122-30.

1041 Pei, Shengji, *et.al.* 'Ethnobotany of Indigenous Nonwood Forest Products in Xishuangpanna of Yunnan in Southwest China', in S.K. Jain (Ed.), *Ethnobiology in Human Welfare: Proceedings of IV International Congress of Ethnobiology, held at Lucknow, India, 1994* (New Delhi: Deep Publications, 1996), pp. 415-23.

1042 Tian, Ghouzong and Raychaudhuri, S.P. 'Paulownia Witches' Broom Diseases in China: Present Status', in S.P. Raychaudhuri and Karl Maramorosch (Eds.), *Forest Trees and Palms: Diseases and Control* (New Delhi: Oxford and IBH Publishing Company, 1996), pp. 227-51.

1043 Wang, Sujuan. 'Biotechnological Study of Seaweeds in China', in Sujuan Wang, *Aquaculture Research Needs for 2000 A.D.* (New Delhi: Oxford and IBH Publishing Company, 1992), pp. 225-28.

1044 Zeyong, X., et.al. 'Current Research on Groundnut Virus Diseases in China', in D.V.R. Reddy and C.L.L. Gowda (Eds.), *Groundnut Virus Diseases in the Asia-Pacific Region: Summary and Recommendations of the Fourth Meeting of the International Working Ground, Mar, 1995, Khon Kaean University, Thailand* (Patancheru, A.P.: International Crops Research Institute for the Semi-Arid Tropics, 1996), pp. 26-27.

- CHEMISTRY

1045 Craddock, Paul T. 'Traditional Zinc Distillation in India and China', in M.C. Ganorkar and N. Rama Rao (Eds.), *International Colloquium on Role of Chemistry in Archaeology (Ist: 1991: Hyderabad, India), Ist International Colloquium on Role of Chemistry in Archaeology, 15-18 November 1991* (Hyderabad: Birla Institute of Scientific Research, 1991), pp. 112-20.

1046 Kuang, Shi-jun. 'The Effluent Treatment Situation and Prospects of Small Paper Mills in China', in UNIDO and Central Pulp and Paper Research Institute, *Proceedings of the International Workshop on Small Scale Chemical Recovery, High Yield Pulping and Effluent Treatment, 1991, New Delhi* (Saharanpur: Central Pulp and Paper Research Institute, 1991), pp. 246-50.

1047 Liu, Hongyun. 'Electrolytic Hydrogen Potential in China', in Asian and Pacific Centre for Transfer of Technology, New Delhi, *Hydrogen Energy: Expert Group Meeting at Kathmandu, Nepal, 1992* (New Delhi: Asian and Pacific Centre for Transfer of Technology, 1993), pp. 73-77.

1048 Zou, Pei Chang. 'The Alkali Recovery System for Black Liquor Based on 50TPD Bleached Straw Pulp', in UNIDO and Central Pulp and Paper Research Institute, *Proceedings of the International Workshop on Small Scale Chemical Recovery, High Yield Pulping and Effluent*

Treatment, 1991, New Delhi (Saharanpur: Central Pulp and Paper Research Institute, 1991), pp. 16-31.

- ENGINEERING

1049 Chen, Chun-Chung and Liang, Wen-Sheng. 'Rehabilitation of Akungtien Reservoir in Taiwan' in C.V.J. Varma and A.R.G. Rao (Eds.), *2nd International Conference: Dam Safety Evaluation November 26-30, Trivandrum, India* (New Delhi: Oxford and IBH Publishing Company, 1996), Vol. 1, pp. 377-84.

1050 Zhang, Sinsheng. 'Dam Construction in China', in Sinsheng Zhang, *Innovative Construction of Water Resources Projects in Asian Region* (New Delhi: Central Board of Irrigation and Power, 1992), pp. 1-13.

- ENVIRONMENTAL STUDIES

1051 Gupta, R.K. 'Some Important Cases, Bisphenol-A From Japan, Isobuty l Benzene From the People's Republic of China, and so on', in R.K. Gupta, *Anti-Dumping and Counter vailing Measures, The Complete Reference* (New Delhi: Response Books, 1996), pp. 154-68.

1052 Hati, A.K. 'Environment and Epidemiology of Japanese Encephalitis in West Bengal', in Salil K. Raha, *et.al.* (Eds.), *Modern Trends in Environmental Biology: Proceedings of a Symposium Held in R.K.M.V., W.B.* (Jaipur: Arihant Publishing House, 1995), pp. 16-21.

1053 Kuang, Shi-jun. 'R and D Achievements in Environmental Aspects of Pulp and Paper Industry of China in Past Years, in UNIDO and Central Pulp and Paper Research Institute, *Proceedings of the International Workshop on Small Scale Chemical Recovery, High Yield Pulping and Effluent Treatment, 1991, New Delhi* (Saharanpur: Central Pulp and Paper Research Institute, 1991), pp. 314-18.

1054 Nomiyama, K. 'Health Effects of Environmental Contamination in Japan—A Historical Review', in T.C. Heetchinson, *et.al.* (Eds.), *Global Perspectives on Lead, Mercury and Cadmium Cyding in the Environment* (New Delhi: New Age International, Wiley Eastern, 1994), pp. 287-96.

1055 Ohta, Takeshi. 'Water Balance and Seasonal Variation of Evapo-Transpiration in the Tanggula Mountains, Tibetan Plateau, Headwater of Yangtze River', in R.B. Singh and Martin J. Haig (Eds.), *Sustainable Reconstruction of Highland and Highwater Regions: Proceedings of Third International Symposium on Headwater Control, New Delhi, October 6-8, 1995* (New Delhi: Oxford and IBH Publishing Company, 1995), pp. 213-20.

1056 Saxena, S.K. 'Japan', in *Cooperatives and Environment: An International Perspective* (Delhi: Pragati Publications, 1995), pp. 34-46.

1057 Shapiro, H.A. 'Environmental Planning for Coastal Regions on the Pacific Rim: Japanese Experience Applied to China', in Mohammad Shafi and Mehdi Raza (Eds.), *Geography of Environment* (Jaipur: Rawat Publications, 1994), pp. 311-46.

1058 Squires, V.R. 'Management and Monitoring of Fragile Ecosystems in the Arid North-West of China, Development of a Silva-Pastoral Ecosystem', in Punjab Singh, *et.al.* (Eds.), *Agroforestry Systems for Sustainable Land Use* (New Delhi: Oxford and IBH Publishing Company, 1994), pp. 121-32.

1059 *Tibet: Environment and Development Issues, 1992* (Dharamsala: Department of Information and International Relations, Central Tibetan Administration of His Holiness the Dalai Lama, 1992).

1060 Zhou, J.Y. 'Speciation and Transfer of Mercury and Arsenic in Surface Sea Water and Marine Environments in China', in T.C. Heetchinson, *et.al.* (Eds.), *Global Perspectives on Land, Mercury and Cadmium Cyding in the Environment* (New Delhi: New Age International, Wiley Eastern, 1994), pp. 131-47.

- HYDROLOGY

1061 Ohta, Takeshi. 'Water Balance Based on the Hydrological Observations in the Tanggula Mountains, the Tibetan Plateau', in R.B. Singh, Martin J. Haig (Eds.), *Sustainable Reconstruction of Highland and Highwater Regions: Proceedings of Third International Symposium on Headwater Control, New Delhi, October 6-8, 1995* (New

Delhi: Oxford and IBH Publishing Company, 1995), pp. 221-24.

- MEDICINE

1062 Anmin, W. 'Theoretical Concepts: Chinese System', in S.N. Tripathi (Ed.), *Medical Systems With a Holistic Approach: Proceedings of a Seminar-Cum-Workshop, New Delhi, 1990* (Varanasi: S.N. Tripathi Memorial Foundation, 1993), pp. 79-88.

1063 Ban, Sadayuki and Sugahara, Tsatomu. 'Radiosensitivity of Skin Fibroblasts and Lymphosytes From Atomic Bomb Survivors in Hiroshima', in D. Bhattacharjee and B.B. Singh, *Radio-Biological Concepts in Radio Therapy* (New Delhi: Narosa Publishing House, 1995), pp. 82-87 .

1064 Bhagwan Dash. *Encyclopaedia of Tibetan Medicine: Being the Tibetan Text of Rgyudbzi and Sanskrit Restoration of Amrta Hydaya Astanga Gu Byopadesa Tantra and Expositional Translation in English*, (Delhi: Sri Satguru Publications, 1994-95), Vols. 1-4: To be completed in 15 volumes.

1065 Bhagwan Dash. *Pharmacopoeia of Tibetan Medicine* (Delhi: Sri Satguru Publications, 1994).

1066 Bhattacharya, Samarendra. *Acupuncture: Philosopher's Point of View* (Calcutta: Multi Book Agency, 1992).

1067 Dutt, Ashok Kumar. 'Patterns of Medical Facilities in the People's Republic of China', in Jayati Hazare (Ed.), *Health Care Planning in the Developing World* (Calcutta: Jayati Hazra, 1994), pp. 109-23.

1068 Fang, Ru-kang. 'The Geographical Inequalities of Mortality of China', in Jayati Hazare (Ed.), *Health Care Planning in the Developing World* (Calcutta: Jayati Hazra, 1994), pp. 19-29.

1069 Kondo, K. 'Increasing Burdens Due to Neurological Diseases in Japan', in J.S. Chopra and I.M.S. Sawhney (Eds.), *Progress in Neurology* (New Delhi: B.I. Churchill Livingstone, 1995), pp. 178-90.

1070 Kondo, K. 'Intractable Diseases Control Program in Japan', in J.S. Chopra and I.M.S. Sawhney (Eds.),

Progress in Neurology (New Delhi: B.I. Churchill Livingstone, 1995), pp. 222-31.

1071 Krishna Murthy, K. 'China', in K. Krishna Murthy, *Dictionary of Medical Archaeology* (Delhi: Sundeep Prakashan, 1996), pp. 70-74.

1072 Lhamo, S. 'Clinical Concept: Tibetan System', in S.N. Tripathi (Ed.), *Medical Systems With a Holistic Approach: Proceedings of a Seminar-Cum-Workshop, New Delhi, 1990* (Varanasi: S.N. Tripathi Memorial Foundation, 1993), pp. 149-50.

1073 Liang, Dong-Cai and Wang, Chih-chen. 'Dorothy and Insulin Crystallographic Research in China', in Dorthy Crowfoot Hodkin, *The Collected Works of Dorothy Crowfoot Hodkin* (Bangalore: Interline Publishing in Collaboration With Indian Academy of Science, 1994), pp. xxviii-xxxi.

1074 Qiming, R. 'Clinical Concepts: Tibetan System', in S.N. Tripathi (Ed.), *Medical Systems with a Holistic Approach: Proceedings of a Seminar-cum-Workshop, New Delhi, 1990* (Varanasi: S.N. Tripathi Memorial Foundation, 1993), pp. 141-48.

1075 Quasar, N. 'Theoretical Concepts: Tibtan System', in S.N. Tripathi (Ed.), *Medical Systems With a Holistic Approach: Proceedings of a Seminar-cum-Workshop, New Delhi, 1990* (Varanasi: S.N. Tripathi Memorial Foundation, 1993), pp. 69-78.

1076 Said, Hakim Mohammed. 'Traditional Chinese Herbal Drugs in the Light of Scientific Studies', in J.N. Govil (Ed.), *Medicinal Plants: New Vista of Research* (New Delhi: Today and Tomorrow's Printers and Publishers, 1993), Part I, pp. 109-19.

1077 Suganami, Shigeru. 'Ayurveda in Japan', in C.N. Ramachandran, *et.al.* (Eds.), *Critical Spectrum: Lectures on Current Issues* (Mangalagangothri: Mangalore University, 1993), pp. 219-25 .

1078 Women's Feature Service, 'Scorpion Tea for the Sexy in China', in Women's Feature Service, *Aids* (New Delhi: Women's Feature Service, 1994), pp. 24-25.

1079 Zhou, Meiyue and Zheng, Chunhua. 'Aids: China', in Women's Feature Service, *Aids* (New Delhi: Women's Feature Service, 1994), pp. 22-23.

- MINING AND METALLURGY

1080 Mori, Masao. 'Development of Steelmaking Refractories in Japan', in B.N. Ghosh, *et.al.* (Eds.), *International Seminar on Refractories, February 27-29, 1992, Jamshedpur: Seminar Papers/Souvenir* (Jamshedpur: Indian Ceramic Society, Jamshedpur Chapter, 1992), pp. 1-26.

- METEOROLOGY

1081 Guo, Xiaorong. 'A Brief Review of the Studies on the Summer Monsoon in China', in P.K. Das (Ed.), *Recent Advances in Atmospheric Physics* (New Delhi: Indian National Science Academy, 1994), pp. 97-99.

1082 Lin, Yifu. 'Tropical Asia: Lessons From the Chinese Experience', in B.R. Berwale (Ed.), *Hybrid Rice: Food Security in India* (Madras: Macmillan India, 1993), pp. 81-94.

1083 Zeng, Qing-cun. 'East Asian Summer Monsoon—A Case Study', in P.K. Das (Ed.), *Recent Advances in Atmospheric Physics* (New Delhi: Indian National Science Academy, 1994), pp. 81-96.

- PHYSICS

1084 Chauhan, P.K.S. and Singh, V.N. 'Shear Wave Velocity Structure of China Region From Rayleigh Wave Dispersion', in *Proceedings of the Second International Seminar and Exhibition: Geophysics Beyond 2000, 15-20 November, 1996, Hyderabad, India* (Hyderabad: Association of Exploration Geophysicists, Centre of Exploration Geophysics, Osmania University, 1996), pp. 364-66.

1085 Ishii, Tamotsu. 'Recent Developments in Nuclear Fuel Cycle in Japan with Emphasis on Material Recycling', in Indian Chemical Engineering Congress (1995; Kalpakkam, India), *Chemcon '95: Abstracts and Invited Lectures* (Kalpakkam: Indian Institute of Chemical Engineers, Kalapakkam Regional Centre, 1996), pp. xxix-xxxii.

- TECHNOLOGY

1086 Narendra Singh. 'International Status of Research and Development: China and Japan', in Narendra Singh, *Green Vegetation Fractionation Technology* (New Delhi: Oxford and IBH Publishing Company, 1996), pp. 168-69.

1087 Qian, Ying-qian. 'Studies on Biotechnology and Biodiversity Related to Rural Development in China', in M.S. Swaminathan (Ed.), *Ecotechnology and Rural Employment: A Dialogue* (Madras: Macmillan, 1994), pp. 218-23.

1088 Zhao, Chunshan and Sun, Jiankin. 'Strengthening Cooperation for Promoting Commercialisation of R&D Results in the Region', in S.N. Sharma and Sundeep Kumar (Eds.), *Report: Asia-Pacific Regional Workshop on R&D Community Enterprise Cooperation in Technological Research and Commercialisation of Results, 7-10 November 1994, New Delhi, India* (New Delhi: Asian and Pacific Centre for Transfer of Technology, 1995), pp. 85-90.

1089 Zhihong, L. 'High-Output and High-Efficiency in Coal Mines of China', in A.K. Sahay, *et.al.* (Eds.), *High Production Technology for Underground Mines* (Calcutta: Mining, Geological Metallurgical Institute of India, 1996), pp. 315-32.

-- Construction Technology

1090 Mittal, K.M. 'Burner Designs Commonly Used in China', in K.M. Mittal, *Biogas Systems: Principles and Applications* (New Delhi: New Age International, 1996), pp. 254-56.

1091 Mittal, K.M. 'Common Materials Used in China for Constructing Fixed Dome Biogas Plants', in K.M. Mittal, *Biogas Systems: Principles and Applications* (New Delhi: New Age International, 1996), pp. 133-35.

-- Food Technology

1092 Ono, Kentaro. 'Trends of Aseptic Packaging Japan', in C.P. Natarajan and S. Ranganna (Eds.), *Trends in Food Science and Technology: Proceedings of the Third International Food Convention (IFCON '93), Held During 7th to 12th September 1993 at Mysore* (Mysore: Association of Food Scientists and Technologists, 1995), pp. 867-74.

1093 Yang, Jui-sen. 'Post-Harvest Handling, Storage, Packaging and Marketing of Horticultural Products in Taiwan', in C.P. Natarajan and S. Ranganna (Eds.), *Trends in Food Science and Technology: Proceedings of the Third International Food Convention (IFCON '93), Held During 7th to 12th September 1993 at Mysore* (Mysore: Association of Food Scientists and Technologists, 1995), pp. 402-07.

-- Industrial Technology

1094 Shimokohbe, Akira. 'The State of the Art of Nanometer Motion Control in Japan', in D. Vijayaraghavan (Ed.), *Industrial Measurements and Automation* (Madras: H.C. Kothari Group, Publications Division, 1996), pp. 2-8.

- GEOLOGY

1095 Arai, Zenya and Hirano, Hironuchi. 'Geochemical Study of the Cenomanian-Turonian Boundary Oceanic Anoxic Event in the Northwestern Pacific Forearc Basin', in Ashok Sahni (Ed.), *Cretaceous Stratigraphy and Palaeo-Environments* (Bangalore: Geological Society of India, 1996), pp. 31-50.

1096 Chen, Pei-Ji. 'Freshwater Biogas, Stratigraphic Correlation of Late Cretaceous of China', in Ashok Sahni (Ed.), *Cretaceous Stratigraphy and Palaeo-Environments* (Bangalore: Geological Society of India, 1996), pp. 35-62.

1097 Deng, Xiao. 'Geotemperature Pattern and Geothermal Resources in North China Basin', in Mohan L. Gupta and Makato Yamano (Eds.), *Terrestrial Heat Flow and Geothermal Energy in Asia* (New Delhi: Oxford and IBH Publishing Company, 1995), pp. 407-34.

1098 Furukawa, Yoshitsugu. 'Temperature Structure in the Crust of the Japan Art and the Thermal Effect of Subduction', in Mohan L. Gupta and Makato Yamano (Eds.), *Terrestrial Heat Flow and Geothermal Energy in Asia* (New Delhi: Oxford and IBH Publishing Company, 1995), pp. 203-19.

1099 Higgitt, David L. 'Assessment of Erosion and Sediment Delivery in a Mountainous Subtropical Catchment, Fujian Province, China', in R.B. Singh and Martin J. Haig

(Eds.), *Sustainable Reconstruction of Highland and Highwater Regions: Proceedings of Third International Symposium on Headwater Control, New Delhi, October 6-8, 1995* (New Delhi: Oxford and IBH Publishing Company, 1995), pp. 299-305.

1100 Hsiao, Tsechiang and Zho, Yusheng. 'Development and Application of Coal Injection in Mini-Blast Furnance in China', in Amitava Bandhyopadhyay and M.S. Khan (Eds.), *International Conference on Alternative Routes to Iron and Steel* (Jamshedpur: Indian Institute of Metals and Tata Steel, 1996), Vol. 2, pp. 65-73.

1101 Ireyaina, Jun. 'Case Study of an Active Volcano in Japan: Geothermal Process and Energy of the Yake-dake Volcano, Japan', in Mohan L. Gupta and Makoto Yamano (Eds.), *Terrestrial Heat Flow and Geothermal Energy in Asia* (New Delhi: Oxford and IBH Publishing Company, pp. 493-516.

1102 Jin, Mingxia and Shen, Su. 'Controls of Ore Localisation and Metallogenic Evolution of Tin-Tungsten Deposits in the Mosuoejing Region, Sichuan, China', in B. Dash, *et.al., Vistas in Geological Research: Prof. S. Acharya Felicitation Volume* (Bhubaneshwar: P.G. Department of Geology, Utkal University, 1995), pp. 88-90.

1103 Kadomura, Hiroshi. 'Land Classification and Geomorphological Mapping in Japan', in R.B. Singh, *Research in Geography* (New Delhi: APH Publishing Corporation, 1996), Vol. 1, pp. 3-12.

1104 Khain, V.E. 'Sino-Korea Craton' and 'South China (Yangtze) Platform and Adjoining Massifs', in V.E. Khain, *Historical Geotectonics, Precambrian* (New Delhi: Oxford and IBH Publishing Company, 1996), pp. 49-52.

1105 Li, Tianchi. 'Landslide Disasters and Their Reduction in China', *Dynamics of Mountain Geosystems* (New Delhi: Ashish Publishing House, 1992), pp. 312-23.

1106 Liao, Zhijle. 'The Rehai (Hot Sea) Geothermal System in Tangchong County, Yunnan Province, China', in Mohan L. Gupta and Makoto Yamano (Eds.), *Terrestrial Heat Flow and Geothermal Energy in Asia* (New Delhi: Oxford and IBH Publishing Company, 1995), pp. 389-405.

1107 Okada, Hakuyu. 'Nature and Teetonic Significance of Cretaceous Sediments in the Japanese Islands', in Ashok Sahni (Ed.), *Cretaceous Stratigraphy and Palaeo-environments* (Bangalore: Geological Society of India, 1996), pp. 85-104.

1108 Pearl, Meruyn R. 'Monitoring of Bedload Sediment Production an`d Movement in Small Stream in Hong Kong', in C.V.J. Varma and A.R.G. Rao (Eds.), *Management of Sediment: Philosophy, Aims and Techniques: Sixth International Symposium, River Sedimentation, November 1995, New Delhi, India* (New Delhi: Central Board of Irrigation and Power, Oxford and IBH Publishing Company, 1995), pp. 343-50.

1109 Ren, Xiaofeng. 'Mechanism of "The Peeling"—"Bed Abrasion" Phenomenon in Wei River', in C.V.J. Varma and A.R.G. Rao (Eds.), *Management of Sediment: Philosophy, Aims and Techniques: Sixth International Symposium, River Sedimentation, November 1995, New Delhi, India* (New Delhi: Central Board of Irrigation and Power, Oxford and IBH Publishing Company, 1995), pp. 517-24.

1110 Shen, Xianjia. 'Abnormal Thermal Structure and Related Geothermal Resources of the Tibetan Plateau', in Mohan L. Gupta and Makoto Yamano (Eds.), *Terrestrial Heat Flow and Geothermal Energy in Asia* (New Delhi: Oxford and IBH Publishing Company, 1995), pp. 369-87.

1111 Sun, Zhen-hua, *et.al.* 'Development of Seabuck Thorn and Conservation of Soil in China', in C.V.J. Varma and A.R.G. Rao (Eds.), *Management of Sediment: Philosophy, Aims and Techniques: Sixth International Symposium, River Sedimentation, November 1995, New Delhi, India* (New Delhi: Central Board of Irrigation and Power, Oxford and IBH Publishing Company, 1995), pp. 17-23.

1112 Wang, Jian. 'Geothermal Characteristics of the South China Sea', in Mohan L. Gupta and Makoto Yamano (Eds.), *Terrestrial Heat Flow and Geothermal Energy in Asia* (New Delhi: Oxford and IBH Publishing Company, 1995), pp. 113-28.

1113 Wang, Ji-yang. 'Heat Flow Pattern and Its Implications for Tectonics in the Continental Area in China', in Mohan L. Gupta and Makoto Yamano (Eds.), *Terrestrial Heat Flow and Geothermal Energy in Asia* (New Delhi: Oxford and IBH Publishing Company, 1995), pp. 83-94.

1114 Wang Zhongmin, *et.al.*, 'Palcomagnetic Results From Late Sinian/Early Cambrian Rocks in Guizhou Province, South China Block', in K.V. Subbarao (Ed.), *Magnetism: Rocks to Superconductors, Radhakrishnamurty Volume* (Bangalore: Geological Society of India, 1994), pp. 159-82.

1115 Yamano, Makoto. 'Recent Heat Flow Studies in and Around Japan', in Mohan L. Gupta and Makoto Yamano (Eds.), *Terrestrial Heat Flow and Geothermal Energy in Asia* (New Delhi: Oxford and IBH Publishing Company, 1995), pp. 173-201.

1116 Zhang, Mingming, *et.al.* 'Investigation of Sediment Movement in Changzhou Reach of the Grand Canal', in C.V.J. Varma and A.R.G. Rao (Eds.), *Management of Sediment: Philosophy, Aims and Techniques: Sixth International Symposium, River Sedimentation, November 1995, New Delhi, India* (New Delhi: Central Board of Irrigation and Power, Oxford and IBH Publishing Company, 1995), pp. 337-42.

1117 Zhu, Zhenda. 'Sand Dune Stabilization in China', in A.K. Sen and Amal Kar (Eds.), *Land Degradation and Desertification in Asia and the Pacific Region* (Jodhpur: Scientific Publishers, 1995), pp. 273-93.

- ZOOLOGY

1118 Ishida, Rikizo, *et.al.* 'Stream Restoration for fishes in Japan', in Neil B. Armantrout and Robert J. Wolotira, *Condition of the World's Aquatic Habitats: Proceedings of the World Fisheries Congress, Theme I* (New Delhi: Oxford and IBH Publishing Corporation, 1995), pp. 225-37.

1119 Kodomari, Shigeru. 'Microbial Control of Tea Insect Pests in Japan', in *Tea Tech, 1993: Proceedings of the International Symposium on Tea Science and Human Health, January 11-14, 1993, Calcutta* (Calcutta: Tea Research Association, 1993), pp. 153-65.

1120 Lui, J.Y. 'Perspectives to Shrimp Mariculture Research in China', in *Aquaculture Research Needs for 2000 A.D.* (New Delhi: Oxford and IBH Publishing Corporation, 1992), pp. 103-113.

1121 Tzeng, Wann-Nian. 'Recruitment of Larval and Juvenile Fishes to the Gong-Shy-Tyan River Estnary of Taiwan: Relative Abundance Species Composition and Seasonality', in Neil B. Armantrout and Robert J. Wolotira, *Condition of the World's Aquatic Habitats: Proceedings of the World Fisheries Congress, Theme I* (New Delhi: Oxford and IBH Publishing Corporation, 1995), pp. 360-85.

1122 Zhu, Xiang and Santiapillai. 'Conservation of Elephants in Xi-shuangbanna, China', in J.C. Daniel and Hemant S. Datye (Eds.), *A Week With Elephants: Proceedings of International Seminar on the Conservation of Asian Elephant, June 1993* (Bombay: Bombay Natural History Society; Oxford University Press, 1995), pp. 249-55.

ANNEXURE

DISSERTATIONS AND THESES (DU AND JNU)

ABBREVIATIONS USED		
DCJS	:	Department of Chinese and Japanese Studies
DU	:	University of Delhi
JNU	:	Jawaharlal Nehru University, New Delhi-110 067
MPT	:	M.Phil. Thesis
PDT	:	Ph.D. Thesis

ANTHROPOLOGY AND SOCIOLOGY

-National Minorities

T-1 Chelli, Hari Kumar, Chinese Communist Party's Policy Towards National Minorities: With Special Reference to Xinjiang (New Delhi: Centre For East Asian Studies, JNU, 1990): MPT.

T-2 Kumar, Shivani, China's Policies Towards Its National Minorities (Delhi: DCJS, DU, 1991) : MPT.

-Ethnic Groups

T-3 Priyadarshini, Vandana, A Comparative Study of Some Aspects of The Societies of Ethnic Tibetans of Ladakh and Western Tibet (Delhi: DCJS, DU, 1993) : MPT.

-Social Problems

T-4 Verma, Samir Kumar, Deng's Reform And Corruption in China: A Preliminary Analysis (Delhi: DCJS, DU, 1992): MPT.

-Social Structure

--Women

T-5 Gulati, Manjula, Changing Status of Women in China, 1966 to 1976 (Delhi: DCJS, DU, 1995): MPT.

T-6 Parida, Savita, Half the Sky : A Study of Women of China in the 1980s (Delhi: DCJS, DU, 1992) : MPT.

T-7 V.Sharda, Status of Women in India and Japan: A Study of the Relative Values of Legal and Social Ideals (Delhi: DCJS, DU, 1992): MPT.

COMMUNICATION AND MEDIA

T-8 Basant, Sarmistha Gupta, Portrayal of Women in Media in Post-Mao China (Delhi: DCJS, DU, 1993): MPT.

DEFENCE AND STRATEGY

-Armament And Disarmament

T-9 Singh, Shailendra Kumar, China's Policy of Disarmament Since 1949: A Theoretical Analysis (Delhi: DCJS, DU, 1992): MPT.

-Army/Army Service

T-10 Verma, Sanjay Kumar, Modernization of the PLA: Conceptual and Institutional Variation (New Delhi: School of International Studies, 1992): MPT.

-Defence Policy

T-11 Chawla, Surendra Singh, China's Defence Policy: A Theoretical Analysis of Doctrinal Shifts (Delhi: DCJS, DU, 1990): MPT.

-Military Hardware

T-12 Mohanty, Deba Ranjan, Arms and Influence: China As an Arms Exporter (New Delhi: Centre for International Politics, Organisation and Disarmament, JNU, 1994): MPT.

T-13 Sepahi, Shahram, A Study of Chinese Arms Industry and Exports in the Seventies and the Eighties (New Delhi: Centre for International Politics, Organisation and Disarmament, JNU, 1990): MPT.

-Nuclear Arms/Policy

T-14 Rout, Satyabrate, Pakistan's Nuclear Policy: United States and China As Factors (New Delhi: Centre for South, Central, South East Asian and South-West Pacific Studies, JNU, 1992): MPT.

ECONOMY

-Economic History

T-15 Kalia, Monica, Role of Chinese Entrepreneur In The Development of Modern Industry of China, 19th Century Senario (Delhi: DCJS, DU, 1993): MPT.

T-16 Srivastava, Ritu, Conflict Resolution in Japanese Industry in Post-World War II Era, 1945-1987 (Delhi: DCJS, DU, 1994): MPT.

T-17 Wadhwa, Sangeeta, Worker's Activism in Japan, 1945-1955 (Delhi: DCJS, DU, 1991): MPT.

-Industries and Industrialization

T-18 Desai, Miroo, Rural Industries in China, 1978-88 (New Delhi: School of International Studies, JNU, 1991): MPT.

T-19 Mukhopadhyay, Sujata, Corporate Paternalism in Post-War Japan: A Study of Its Policies and Problems (New Delhi: Centre for East Asian Studies, JNU, 1990): MPT.

T-20 Rajiv Raghunath, The Energy Policies of Japan Since 1979 (New Delhi: Centre for East Asian Studies, JNU, 1990): MPT.

-International Economics

T-21 Ghose, Madanmohan, Structure and Impact of Non-Tariff Trade Barriers: Case Study of India vis-a-vis EEC, Japan and USA (New Delhi: Centre for Studies in Diplomacy, International Law and Economics, JNU, 1993): MPT.

T-22 Sebastain, Thomas, Indo-Japan Trade on Fisheries: Problems and Prospects (New Delhi: Centre for East Asian Studies, JNU, 1993): MPT.

-Public Sector

T-23 Roy Choudhury, Srabany, The Public Sector in Japan—An Assessment of Policy and Programme (New Delhi: Centre for East Asian Studies, JNU, 1990): MPT.

-Trade, Domestic

T-24 Sajeev, K.S., Liberalisation of Trade in China and India : A Comparative Study, 1984-1992 (New Delhi: Centre for East Asian Studies, JNU, 1993): MPT.

EDUCATION

-Educational History

T-25 Mukherjee, Basabi, Japanese Colonial Educational System : A Case Study of Korea and Taiwan (Delhi: DCJS, DU, 1993): MPT.

-Educational Reform

T-26 Mukherjee, Rupali, Knowledge, Power and Reality: An Analysis of Western Construction of the GPCR Educational Reform (Delhi: DCJS, DU, 1994): MPT.

-Higher Education

T-27 Mathur, Nalini, Prelude to the Tiananmen Incident: A Reconstruction of the Educational Scene in the year 1988 (Delhi: DCJS, DU, 1990): MPT.

GEOGRAPHY

T-28 Keliat, Makumur, The South China Sea Disputes: A Case Study of the Spratlys (New Delhi: Centre for South, Central, South-East Asian and South-West Pacific Studies, JNU, 1994): MPT.

HISTORY

-Modern

T-29 Kotiyal, Pramod Shankar, Yoshida Shigeru and Japan's Postwar Reconstruction, 1945-1954 (Delhi: DCJS, DU, 1990): MPT.

T-30 Pandey, Kiran, China's Entry into the Korean War: Decision, Strategy and Consequences (Delhi: DCJS, DU, 1995): MPT.

INTERNATIONAL RELATIONS

CHINA

-Asia, East

--Taiwan

T-31 Mathew, Sebastian, The Changing Attitude of the PRC Towards Taiwan (New Delhi: School of International Studies, JNU, 1992): MPT.

-Asia, South

--India

T-32 Chauhan, Rakhee, Sino-Indian Boundary Dispute in the Western Sector, 1842-1963 (Delhi: DCJS, DU, 1992): MPT.

T-33 Ekka, Kanti Kumar, Tibet As a Factor in India-China Relations, 1976-1993 (New Delhi: Centre for South, Central and South-East Asia and South-West Pacific Studies, JNU, 1994): MPT.

T-34 Geeta Bharati, The Sino-Indian Border in the Central Sector: Historical Background and the Problem, C.900 to 1962 (Delhi: DCJS, DU, 1993): MPT.

T-35 Jha, Sindhu Kumar, India-China Border Dispute: The Major Issues (New Delhi: Centre for South, Centre, South-East Asian and South-West Pacific Studies, JNU, 1990): MPT.

T-36 Madhok, Shakti, The Soviet Union and India's Territorial Claims in the Sino-Indian Border Dispute (Delhi: DCJS, DU, 1990): MPT.

T-37 Mishra, Keshav, India and China: Normalisation of Relations in the Eighties (New Delhi: Centre for South, Central, South-East Asian and South-West Pacific Studies, JNU, 1992): MPT.

T-38 Saklani, Avinash Mohan, The Visit of Premier Zhou Enlai in April 1960 and Drift Towards War (Delhi: DCJS, DU, 1993): MPT.

T-39 Santosh, The Sino-Indian Border in the North-East, 1914-1962: The Background and the Problem (Delhi DCJS, DU, 1991): MPT.

T-40 Yadav, Shyama Prasad, Soviet Reactions to Indian's Normalisation of Relations With China and Pakistan (New Delhi: Centre for Soviet and East European Studies, JNU, 1992): PDT.

--Nepal

T-41 Ashok Kumar, The Evolution of the Sino-Nepalese Boundary (Delhi: DCJS, DU, 1990): MPT.

--Pakistan

T-42 Bhutia, Mirap Dojee, China-Pakistan Relations, 1949-71 : A National Interest Analysis (Delhi: DCJS, DU, 1991): MPT.

T-43 Yadav, Dinesh, Sino-Pak Relations, 1960-1985 (Delhi: DCJS, DU, 1990): MPT.

-Asia, South-east

T-44 Nanda, Girija Bhusan, Thai Perception and Policy Towards China, 1975-1991 (New Delhi: Centre for South, Central, South-east Asian and South-west Pacific Studies, JNU, 1993): MPT.

-Europe

T-45 Chandrasekharan, A, China-EEC Relations: 1980-1989 (New Delhi: Centre for East Asian Studies, JNU, 1990): MPT.

T-46 Panigrahi, Biranchi Narayan, Sino-West German Relations, 1972-1990 (New Delhi: Centre for East Asian Studies, JNU, 1992): MPT.

--Soviet Union

T-47 Abhay Singh, Issues in Sino-Soviet Dispute, 1956-1976 (New Delhi: Centre for Soviet and East European Studies, JNU, 1990): MPT.

T-48 Pattnaik, Soumyajit, Soviet Policy Towards China During the Gorbachev Period (New Delhi: Centre for Soviet and East European Studies, JNU, 1990): MPT.

JAPAN

-USA

T-49 Chattopadhyay, Sonali, SDI And Japan (New Delhi: Centre for American and West European Studies, JNU, 1990): MPT.

LAW

T-50 Uma Devi, Legal Provisions and Women's Right : A Study of the Two Marriage Laws of the People's Republic of China (Delhi: DCJS, DU, 1990): MPT.

LITERATURE

T-51 Bajpai, Divya, A Comparative Study of Two Dystopias: `Gulliver's Travels' of Jonathan Swift and `City of Cats' of Lao She (Delhi: DCJS, DU, 1995): MPT.

PHILOSOPHY AND RELIGION

T-52 Puneeta Kala, A Study of New Religious Thought and Movements in Japan (New Delhi: Centre of East Asian Studies, JNU, 1993): MPT.

POLITICS AND GOVERNMENT

Political Freedom

T-53 Chakravorty, Meena, Chinese Government's Response to Prodemocratic Movements, 1978-1989 (Delhi: DCJS, DU, 1993): MPT.

T-54 D'Cruz, S.Kumar, The Debate on Democracy in the Post-Mao China (Delhi: DCJS, DU, 1994): MPT.

T-55 Guite, Esther Ching, Struggle For Democracy In China, 1979-1989 (Delhi: DCJS, DU, 1990): MPT.

T-56 Sharma, Sharmila, Reconstruction and Reevaluation of the Student Movement of April-June 1989 in China (Text in Hindi) (Delhi: DCJS, DU, 1991): MPT.

T-57 Singh, Uday Pratap, Tiananmen Square Massacre and the Issue of Human Rights: U.S. Perception (New Delhi: Centre for American and West European Studies, JNU, 1993): MPT.

-Political Ideology

T-58 Sanjay Kumar, A Comparative Study of Mass Mobilization and the Ideology of Gandhi in India, 1945-48, and of Mao in China (Delhi: DCJS, DU, 1995): MPT.

T-59 Suresh, T.G., The Concept of `Transition Period' in Mao Zedong's Thought (New Delhi: Centre for East Asian Studies, JNU, 1993): MPT.

T-60 Yadav, Suraj, Nationalism and Chinese Communism: An Analysis of the Thought of Mao Ze-dong (Delhi: DCJS, DU, 1990): MPT.

-Political Parties

T-61 Divakara Rao, Y.V.S., The Japanese Communist Party: Recent Developments (Delhi: DCJS, DU, 1990): MPT.

T-62 Subair, A., The Communist Party of China and Soviet Revisionism : The Albanian Factor (New Delhi: School of International Studies, JNU, 1991): MPT.

-Political Structure

T-63 Shuya, Pfulhoatuo, Evolution of the State Structure in China: With Special Reference To the Post-Mao Period (Delhi: DCJS, DU, 1992): MPT.

-Revolution And Revolutionary Movements

T-64 Alpana, Awasti, Role of the Red Guards During the Cultural Revolution (Delhi: DCJS, DU, 1993): MPT.

T-65 Chatterjee, Sofia, Soong Ching Ling and the Chinese Revolution (Delhi: DCJS, DU, 1994): MPT.

T-66 Kakkar, Jaya, Mao's Cultural Revolution: Economic Model (Delhi: DCJS, DU, 1994): MPT.

T-67 Murgai, Samriti, The Great Proletarian Cultural Revolution: A Critical Assessment (Delhi: DCJS, DU, 1993): MPT.

T-68 Singh, Raj Kumar, The Role of the Westerners in the Self-Strengthening Movement in China, 1960s-1990s (Delhi: DCJS, DU, 1994): MPT.

SCIENCE AND TECHNOLOGY

T-69 Skehar, D. Varaprasad, Science and Ideology in Deng's China (New Delhi: Centre of East Asian Studies, JNU, 1993): MPT.

End Note: In order to obtain complete and up-to-date information on Theses and Dissertations approved by the University of Delhi, refer to the following source:

Kumar, B.K., Department of Chinese and Japanese Studies, University of Delhi, M.Phil. and Ph.D. Dissertations 1977-97 (Delhi: Department of Chinese and Japanese Studies, DU, February 1998)

AUTHOR INDEX

L

SUBJECT INDEX